England Rugby World Champions

England Rugby World Champions

Celebrating a Golden Year

Foreword by
Rob Andrew

Edited by Philip Brown
Text by Hugh Godwin

MITCHELL BEAZLEY

Page 2 Jason Robinson celebrates scoring a try in the Rugby World Cup final against Australia.

Contents page The England pack control a maul against Uruguay in their Pool C match in the World Cup.

England Rugby World Champions
Edited by **Philip Brown**

Copyright © Octopus Publishing Group Ltd 2004

First published in Great Britain by Mitchell Beazley
An imprint of Octopus Publishing Group Ltd,
2–4 Heron Quays, London E14 4JP

Executive Editor **Vivien Antwi**
Design **Vivienne Brar**
Managing Editor **Mark Fletcher**
Production **Gary Hayes**
Copy-editor **Henry Russell**
Proofreader **John Mapps**
Indexer **Sue Farr**

A CIP record for this book is available from the British Library

ISBN 1 84533 054 4

Repro by Bright Arts (Hong Kong) Ltd
Printed and bound in Italy

Contents

Foreword
by Rob Andrew

The photographs in this book provide a powerful, vivid and colourful recollection of an extraordinary period in English rugby union, and in the sport as a whole.

I was in Australia for the final weeks of the 2003 World Cup, working for BBC Radio, and it was almost beyond description for someone as close to the game as I am. I felt as a player in the early 1990s that it would work as a professional sport, and here was the proof.

The semi-final between England and France was sensational in its own right. To be with 40,000 English supporters in a stadium in Sydney, 12,000 miles from home, was an experience which will never leave me. Then we endured the most remarkable drama in the final, which ended of course with Jonny Wilkinson doing what we've all dreamed of doing since the age of six or seven. It was almost like it was destined to happen. In my opinion, Martin Johnson deserved to lift the World Cup, simply because his status and achievements demanded he should be a World Cup-winning captain.

I have often been asked about my scream of delight during the radio commentary at the final when Jonny dropped the winning goal. Take a look at Jonny's face in the photos which capture the moments of victory, and you'll get a good idea of what was going on in my mind, too. I played with him in his early days at Newcastle, and have watched him grow from the teenager he was when he signed for us. I was also in a team which lost a final to Australia, at Twickenham in 1991, and it still haunts most of us who played. So it came out of emotion for the team, and for Jonny. Being so close to him, knowing how much he'd put into it, and knowing how close England had got 12 years before. You never know when you will get the chance again. Everything can change.

An enormous amount of effort and thought went into England's success. They probably peaked in Melbourne at the start of the year covered by this book, but they were the best side at the tournament proper, and they had the strength, togetherness and ability to win it. They also had up to 10 genuinely world class players, as any team must have to win a world championship. As we have seen since the World Cup, it is extremely difficult to produce the right formula. In the 2004 Six Nations Championship, marginal victories suddenly became marginal defeats. But that is sport, and that is rugby, and there is no need to dwell on the negative.

We are entering a new era. Fame is not something Jonny wanted but he is learning to deal with it. The media hype is part of modern-day life, and one consequence is the presence of the battalion of photographers who have contributed to this book. We will create the odd icon, and it is part of the evolution of rugby. The pictures from the victory parade in Trafalgar Square sum up for me not only that rugby has always been a big sport in this country, internationally at least, but also my deep belief that sport is important to this nation across the spectrum, from grass roots level upwards.

I believe we are developing young players and supporters who have phenomenal values we should all be proud of. In Newcastle we have people who never watched rugby before, who are now going to cup finals and England matches at Twickenham, and are becoming part of the rugby family.

That is the England team's legacy from an amazing year, and it is justifiably a cause for celebration.

The England captain, Martin Johnson, celebrates with the Webb Ellis Cup after winning the World Cup final.

Sir Clive Woodward and the England
team with the Webb Ellis Cup
aboard the open-topped bus
during the victory parade
through the streets of London.

Introduction

From its foundation in 1871 rugby union was officially defined by its amateur ethos. The principle of the game being played for fun and recreation, and never for money, was enshrined in its constitution. In reality, however, unchecked under-the-counter payments were made for years before the International Rugby Board, the world governing body, declared the game open in 1995. Henceforth players and coaches could legitimately be paid for their involvement.

England entered the brave new world uncertainly. The demise of shamateurism was broadly welcomed there, as was the transfer of power from the old administrators, who were widely regarded as stuffed shirts, to the most important people in the game, the players. There were, however, fears that professionalism would erode the traditional Corinthian values – a certain standard of behaviour on the field, unswerving loyalty to team-mates and a healthy respect for authority – to the detriment of the game.

The trick would be to merge the old with the new. Perhaps paradoxically, given the association the governing body had formerly made between competition and professionalism, rugby had instituted a World Cup in 1987. The tournament was instigated by the powers of the southern hemisphere: mainly New Zealand and Australia, but also South Africa, even though at the time it was still in sporting isolation. The All Blacks of New Zealand won the first World Cup, Australia's Wallabies won the second in 1991 and the Springboks from South Africa, who had been readmitted to the fold on the abolition of apartheid, took the third in 1995. Australia's repeat triumph in 1999 made it 4–0 to the southern hemisphere.

England's World Cup record, as in football and cricket, was largely undistinguished. The country that gave the world the game appeared in only one of the first four finals – on their own ground at Twickenham in 1991 – and had been knocked out in two quarter-finals and a semi-final. Wales did for them in Australia in 1987; in the 1995 semi-finals they lost to an All Blacks' side inspired by giant wing Jonah Lomu, who scored four tries; in 1999 five dropped goals from South Africa's fly-half Jannie de Beer put an end to English hopes in the last eight. It was a pretty poor showing by the Union with the largest playing population on the planet, spread among its 2,000 member clubs. There were many reasons for England's lack of success, but high on the list was the conservative attitude of the people who used to run English rugby. Whereas in the southern hemisphere – even in Australia, where rugby union is strictly a minority sport – everything was geared to international success, the English preoccupation with amateurism survived into the open era and often seemed to undermine the national team.

There had been periods when things went right. In the years before and after the Great War, England were pre-eminent. In the 1970s there were notable one-off victories away to South Africa and New Zealand, but Wales held sway in the annual Five Nations Championship. Conversely, in the early 1990s, England under their charismatic captain, Will Carling, were successful on the home front with three Grand Slams, but made little impact in the southern hemisphere. The nation at that time could turn out plenty of tough and capable forwards, but men such as Wade Dooley and Dean Richards also had day jobs in the police, and regarded themselves as disadvantaged against the quasi-professionals who represented the southern hemisphere. Always there, too, were France, more or less on a par with England in terms of available cash and playing numbers.

By appointing Clive Woodward as their first full-time coach in September 1997 the England Rugby Football Union made a statement of intent. They put their faith in a 41-year-old former Leicester, England and British & Irish Lions player with a background in business and a slim yet burgeoning coaching CV. Woodward was always going to do things differently, for better or worse. Players coached by him at Henley, London Irish and, for a short spell, Bath, testified to his imaginative ways. Just as often, there were tales of his maverick behaviour. Woodward's team selection and tactics baffled many people, who concluded that he based them on which side of the bed he had got out of that morning.

Old school he wasn't. With a 1980s flair for management techniques, honed during five years in Sydney, and a 1990s rage at England's habit of losing to southern hemisphere sides, Woodward set about a revolution. The way he treated his players was partly inspired by Paddy Lund, a radical dentist in Brisbane who took a saw to his receptionist's desk and replaced it with a coffee bar. Plain old patients became valued clients; they were made to feel special and looked forward to their dates with the drill. Woodward reasoned that his players were eager to play for England – for most it was their greatest ambition – but more was needed to inspire their dedication to the cause. He demanded that they discard the amateur ways of 15 pints and a curry on Saturday night (and every other night in some cases) but made it plain that the sacrifices would be understood and rewarded. "He wanted people to turn up to England training and be blown away," said Lawrence Dallaglio, the back-row forward from Wasps. "For the national team to be on another level, another planet, from your everyday life with your club."

The epitome of the new approach was Jonny Wilkinson. He had been marked out from his pre-teens at Farnham Rugby Club in Surrey as an international prospect, and was given his England debut by Woodward as an 18-year-old in 1998. Wilkinson had known only the professional approach, and his devotion to duty soon earned plenty of attention and admiration outside rugby. If Wilkinson felt like getting the kicking tee out on Christmas Day to practise his shots at goal, no amount of sherry or mince pies would distract him from doing so.

Jason Leonard, the barrel-chested prop with the barrow-boy accent, was one of several members of the squad who had crossed the bridge from amateurism into the open era. "Before, rugby was my hobby, my fun time," said Leonard. "Now, my hobby is my job. Some people are very scared of change. Clive isn't, at all. If anything, he welcomes change."

And the players welcomed Woodward. The likes of Wilkinson, Dallaglio and Leonard joined the captain, Martin Johnson, in a team that went from strength to strength in the four years building up to the fifth World Cup, which would be staged over 48 matches and 41 days in Australia in October and November 2003. The senior figures were unlikely to get another crack at the game's ultimate prize. As they gathered together in the summer of 2003, the England rugby team were fully prepared to take on the world. Their readiness had not happened by accident.

The Webb Ellis Cup.

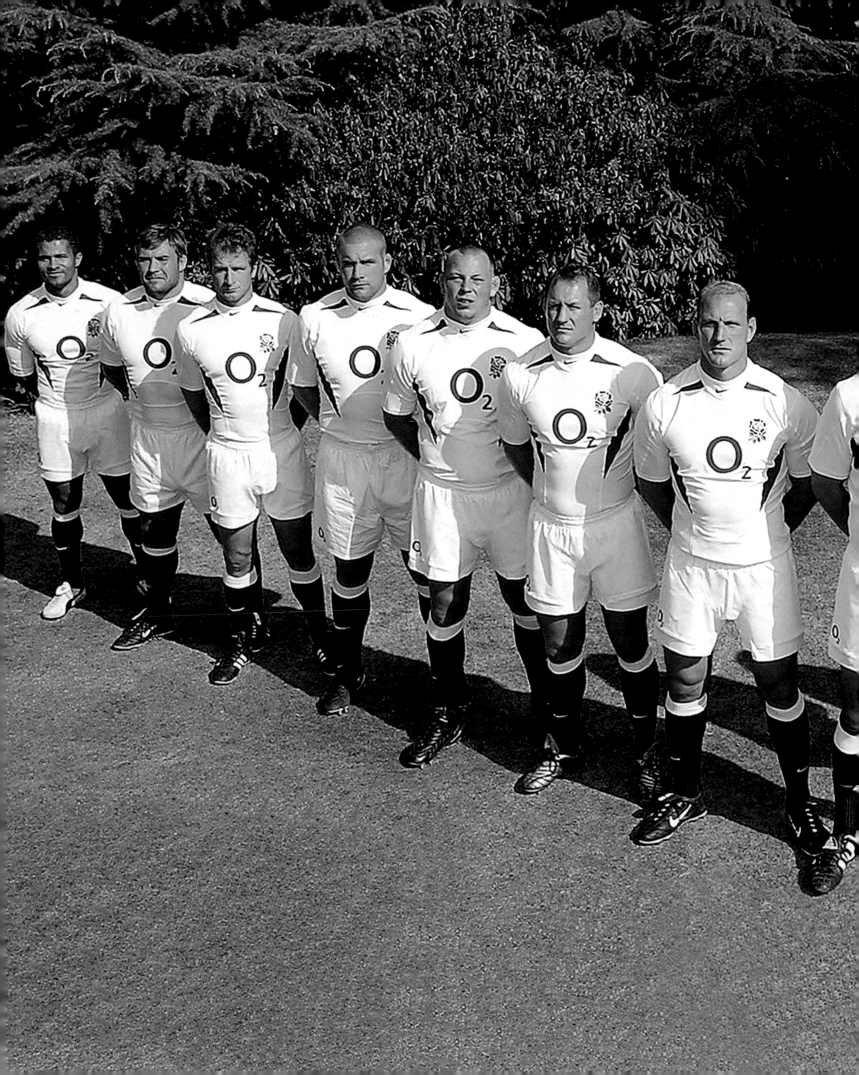

Preparing for the World Cup

Preparing for the World Cup

It must be a perplexing sight for well-heeled businessmen or women, or perhaps American or Japanese tourists seeking the quintessentially English stopover, when they first encounter Pennyhill Park. Turning into the long driveway to their five-star destination in a quiet corner of London's stockbroker belt 30 miles west of the city, they may glance to their left to be greeted by the first evidence that this is no ordinarily opulent country hotel. A set of rugby posts shoots skywards at either end of a lovingly tended training field. And if the England squad happens to be in camp there will also be 30 or 40 very fit, very determined and mostly very large individuals going at it hammer and tongs under the beady eyes of an equally dedicated team of coaches. If the visitors have any appreciation of what these players are about, going through their training drills and fitness routines in this moderately surreal location, they will breathe sighs of relief that their own toughest physical engagement that evening will be the couple of steps into the jacuzzi.

England's rugby team have come to be described as the most dedicated group of sportspeople on the planet, and it is at Pennyhill Park, amid the trees and the faint drone of the traffic on the M3, that a lot of the hard work is done. It was here in the summer of 2003 that Martin Johnson and his men gathered to begin in earnest their challenge for the World Cup. Johnson's side led the International Rugby Board's world rankings, having beaten all their closest rivals in the previous nine months, and were hovering as second or third favourites behind the New Zealand All Blacks and the hosts to win the tournament to be staged in Australia later that year.

Clive Woodward could not recall having received rugby coaching as a schoolboy, even in anything so basic as how to tackle. But he grew into a devotee of the American football system of six coaches of defence and six coaches of attack, with a head coach in overall charge. Woodward tailored this approach to the different needs of rugby – a vastly more fluid game than gridiron – and persuaded the powers-that-be at Twickenham to provide the necessary funding. From the outset, he recruited Phil Larder from rugby league to scrutinise England's defence; in 2000, former Bath and England player Andy Robinson took charge of the forwards in place of New Zealander John Mitchell. By the time the World Cup preparations were in full swing, Woodward had the following staff in place: Robinson (coach/forwards), Larder (assistant coach/defence), Dave Alred (kicking coach), Dave Reddin (fitness), Phil Keith-Roach (scrummaging), Simon Hardy (line-out throwing), Sherylle Calder (visual awareness), Tony Biscombe (video analyst), Simon Kemp (doctor), Phil Pask (physiotherapist), Richard Wegrzyk (masseur), David Tennison (kit technician), Barney Kenny (physiotherapist) and Louise Ramsay (team manager).

It was this kind of extensive support system that enabled Lawrence Dallaglio to spend the best part of a year recovering from a serious knee injury. Dallaglio trained both at his club, Wasps, and at Twickenham under Reddin. If it had been the amateur era he might have given up the game. This way, he was able to come back fitter and stronger than ever.

First-class travel on aeroplanes was another Woodward innovation. No longer would 6ft 9in lock forwards have to scrape their chins on their knees

Previous pages The England Rugby squad line up at a media day at the Pennyhill Park hotel near London. Left to right: Jason Robinson, Jason Leonard, Mike Catt, Phil Vickery, Steve Thompson, Richard Hill, Lawrence Dallaglio, Martin Johnson, Ben Kay, Ben Cohen, Josh Lewsey, Matt Dawson, Neil Back, Jonny Wilkinson, Will Greenwood.

Above England celebrate winning the Grand Slam after beating Ireland 42–6 at Lansdowne Road, Dublin, in March 2003.

Jason Leonard and Trevor Woodman in an ice bath at Pennyhill Park in Surrey.

on long flights in economy. In 1998, during Woodward's first tour with the senior England squad, he was forced by injuries and withdrawals to take a scratch side on the toughest of trips around the southern hemisphere. When they reached what Woodward deemed a sub-standard hotel in Cape Town, South Africa, he marched his men out of the front door and into a more desirable residence up the road, all funded by a swipe of his own credit card. To some it may have appeared a flash gesture. The players, nearing the end of an arduous tour of seven defeats in seven matches, appreciated what had been done on their behalf. You cannot buy loyalty, but you can inspire it through the correct words and deeds. "I wanted to move the image of rugby union away from pints of beer with the lads down the pub," said Woodward. "The image of rugby union should be as the most professional sport in the world."

Woodward moved England out of their former base at Bisham Abbey. Up went the posts at Pennyhill Park, and the team's expectations went the same way. In their oak-panelled bedrooms, players had notes slipped under the door each evening, setting out the training regime for the following day. They were each given a laptop computer, enabling Woodward to communicate instructions by e-mail whenever he needed to. The blazers at the Rugby Football Union (RFU) who told the coach he would be better off supplying his players with "raw meat" were politely ignored.

Jonny Wilkinson described the ambience painstakingly created by the coach: "When the euphoria of being with England died down and you went back to your club, you couldn't bear the thought of not being there the next time." In a variation on the old adage "take care of the pennies and the pounds will look after themselves", Woodward attended to what he called "the critical non-essentials". He said: "You don't win a Test match because you're got better clothes than the All Blacks, or you arrive in a bus with a big England rose on it. But when you add up all these hundreds of things, that's why you do win."

England's most capped player, Jason Leonard, could hold his own with Dylan Thomas and Brendan Behan in every sense other than possibly the literary one. He did not suddenly become a supplement-taking automaton. What Leonard and the rest of the squad did was agree on a set of standards below which, if one fell, they all fell. The rules were written down in a black book. Punctuality for team meetings, for instance, meant arriving 10 minutes ahead of the arranged time. "If a player did come late," said Woodward, "I wouldn't tell him he was late, I'd tell him he'd cost us the World Cup." Will Greenwood, who like Leonard had both the talent and the temperament to have flourished perfectly well in the old amateur era, said: "Clive provided the facilities to help good players become great players; the coaching staff, the hotels, the kit, every little thing."

The danger of becoming too cosseted, of players abusing the life of luxury, was never a problem. The peer pressure among rugby players is immense. Anyone not pulling his weight – or indeed pushing his weights in the bespoke fitness centre erected next to the Pennyhill Park training field – would quickly find himself ostracised. Johnson, the beetle-browed captain from Leicester, was an ideal figurehead: uncompromising on the field and with the media; good-humoured, popular and, above all, highly respected by his fellow players. Woodward defined those who didn't fit in as "energy-sappers". A high-profile casualty was Richard Cockerill, an all-action hooker and former club-mate of Johnson who criticised the coach's methods in a book. Cockerill was the sort who would and sometimes did shed blood for England, but for his perceived misdemeanour he was dropped from the squad, never to return. The message was clear: united, we stand; divided is not an option.

The fitness centre soon became known among the players as "The Church". Here they sang from the hymn sheet that was Dave Reddin's personalised workout programme, and worshipped at the altar of physical exercise in a white prefab building that resembled a marquee at a wedding reception. Rowing machines, free weights, a couple of track hurdles to practise standing jumps – it had all the paraphernalia of a top gymnasium. Sessions began at 7 a.m., before the thermometer mercury could rise to its sweltering midsummer highs. Reddin worked with nutritionists Adam Carey and Matt Lovell to create a diet rich in protein rather than carbohydrates. "I remember at schoolboy level we used to have chicken and chips before a game," laughed Andy Gomarsall, one of England's three scrum-halves. "It wouldn't happen now. The normal pre-match meal is as simple as possible: sandwiches, spaghetti bolognese, boiled chicken." Sherylle Calder had the players exercising their eye muscles for 20 minutes a day. "We analyse blood, hair, all sorts of things," said Reddin. "I'm not flogging the players to death just for the sake of it. There's scientific reasoning behind everything we do."

The Warm-up Plan

There was speculation in some quarters that front-line players such as Johnson and Wilkinson would be better off spending the first part of the summer on the beach, rather than engaged in hand-to-hand combat with a bunch of snarling All Blacks and Wallabies in their respective backyards. Woodward and his chief lieutenant, Andy Robinson, reasoned precisely the opposite. Robinson, a former back-row forward, was no shrinking violet. The only thing violet about him was the shade his cheeks would turn if anything less than maximum effort was put in by his charges. The two men were allowed to pick 30 players for the World Cup. They had in mind all but half a dozen, and wanted to test their first choice line-up in a couple of dress rehearsals before the curtain rose.

Here Woodward learned from harsh experience. Four years earlier, although he had worked his squad hard in training – perhaps even harder than the current crop – the match practice before the 1999 World Cup had been gentle to the point of barely breaking a sweat. England cantered through four warm-up games barely worthy of the name against Canada, the USA and two teams of inaptly-named Premiership Allstars. It was not the only reason England slumped to defeat by South Africa in the quarter-finals of the '99 tournament, but Woodward concluded that it was a significant factor.

For 2003, Woodward arranged a fixture programme that would have been tougher only if he had chucked in 15 rounds with Lennox Lewis. Assembling at Pennyhill Park on 1 June, England were to play full Tests

Jonny Wilkinson throws a pass during a training session at Pennyhill Park in September.

against New Zealand in Wellington and Australia in Melbourne, kicking off the three-week trip with a scarcely less exacting Monday-night jaunt for the fringe candidates to New Plymouth to face a physically strong Maori side.

Those games were followed by a fact-finding trip to Perth – the England base for the first phase of the World Cup – before a return to Blighty for three months of training, punctuated by occasional days off. The programme concluded with another trio of preparatory fixtures on successive Saturdays in August and September against Wales in Cardiff, then back-to-backs with France in Marseilles and Twickenham.

They travelled first class, and they travelled as champions of the northern hemisphere, having ended the 2003 domestic season by winning their first Grand Slam in nine years. It would not have been a mortal wound to head down under – either for the short tour or for the main event in October – without the title, but it could well have been damaging to morale. Woodward's side needed to rebuff critics who claimed that, despite regular victories, they were "bottlers" on the biggest occasions. "If we don't win the Grand Slam next year," Dallaglio had said after finishing second in the 2002 Six Nations, "then we should probably be all lined up and disposed of." The firing squad was not needed. England were utterly dominant in winning the conclusive match against Ireland 42–6 in Dublin, and Johnson, as captain, collected the Six Nations title, the Triple Crown and that much-anticipated Slam. Nevertheless, Woodward typically kept the lid on the celebrations. He had bigger fish to fry. "It has never been a monkey on the back to me," he said of the Slam. "We have learnt our lessons brilliantly well and we will keep learning. This is a great boost for us in 2003 – it puts a spring in the step." Later he said: "I made it clear to the players that the only reason I was doing this job was not to win the Grand Slam or whatever, but to be the best in the world."

The June Tour

No country on earth can rival New Zealand for its love of rugby. Arriving at Auckland airport in June 2003, the first question you were asked was not "Have you anything to declare?" but "Do you reckon the Poms have got a chance?" The locals know their stuff, and are not afraid to tell you, and all but the most blindly patriotic knew that Johnson's team were serious contenders. *The Herald* newspaper failed to find any obvious chinks in England's armour, and so had a go at the team's physical appearance, describing their forwards as "gargoyles". This at least gave the team a foretaste of the treatment they would receive from the press and broadcast media in Australia. The squad used a day off to visit the set of the film *Lord of the Rings: The Return of the King*. Perhaps it was a tribute to Johnson, who had played in New Zealand in his formative years. One Kiwi wag was inspired by the tales of Mordor to dub Johnson's men "white orcs on steroids".

The Test match itself was deadly serious. England were determined to justify their world No. 1 ranking. On the morning of the game, visiting reporters staying in the England hotel in the centre of Wellington queued for breakfast with the players and noticed one of the starting XV shaking like a leaf as he collected his plate. Lawrence Dallaglio stepped in with a steadying hand. By the evening, there was a telling tingle in the air at the

Clive Woodward with the England players during a training session at Pennyhill Park.

Westpac Stadium, otherwise known as the Cake Tin because of its simple oval lines, and not all of it was caused by the chill, blustery wind swirling around the ground. High up in a hospitality suite in the stands sat Jonah Lomu, so often the scourge of England, but removed from the fray by a kidney complaint that had forced him onto dialysis. The No. 11 jersey was worn by the much slighter Caleb Ralph. It was New Zealand's first international of their winter season, and the All Blacks' coach, John Mitchell – the erstwhile assistant to Woodward – had not yet settled on his preferred back line for the World Cup. Similarly, in the back row, Rodney So'oialo was given a chance to stake his claim; a tremendous demand to make of a raw 23-year-old, pittted against England's trio of 50-cap men, Richard Hill, Neil Back and Dallaglio.

Phil Larder had made it his business in the quiet weeks after the Six Nations to tweak the defence that had shipped four tries to the All Blacks at Twickenham the previous November. The intense Lancastrian was itching to see if his adjusted system would work.

At the end of a rather messy first half, Johnson and company had not flagged against their younger opponents, and had thus gone some way to rebutting gibes about their age – the antipodean media had dubbed the England team "Dad's Army". In the third quarter, with England leading 9–6 through three penalties by Wilkinson to two from Carlos Spencer, there was a passage of play which would go down in rugby folklore. First, England lost Back to the sin bin. A couple of minutes later, Dallaglio joined him. New Zealand were awarded a scrum close to the visitors' goal line: the All Blacks' eight would take on England's six. No try can ever be called certain before it is scored, but this was a situation any pack would relish – they would either use their numerical advantage to drive back the opposition, or suck in the defence and score when the inevitable gap opened out wide.

Johnson had neither scenario in mind. The skipper gathered his five remaining fellow forwards around him and told them in typically curt language what was expected. At the first scrum, the front rows stood up and it was re-set. Second scrum: the front rows went down, and it was re-set again. Third scrum: Steve Thompson stood up, and Phil Vickery needed a moment's attention to a blood injury. Fourth scrum: Graham Rowntree stepped out of the scrum: penalty to New Zealand. Losing patience, the All Blacks tapped and ran, only for So'oialo, the inexperienced No. 8, to be held up from scoring by Hill, the proven master of getting his body in where it counts. Not only that but England, having survived two minutes of the most intense pressure, earned a penalty against So'oialo for a double movement. Johnson's craggy features were lit by a huge, taunting grin. Back returned to the field and, at a seven-man scrum, New Zealand were penalised in the front row. Dallaglio trotted on to restore England to the full complement in time to see Wilkinson put over the kick for a barely believable 12–6 lead. Doug Howlett was probably offside as he flew past Dallaglio to score a breakaway try created by Spencer. Finally Wilkinson dropped a goal – another taste of things to come. England won 15–13. Afterwards when loosehead prop Graham Rowntree spoke to reporters outside the official reception in the Te Papa National Museum, the look on his face told that he scarcely believed what he had been a part of.

England, self-critical to a fault, knew that they had got away with it in Wellington. They had not played well, but their defence had held firm. If they could add some attacking thrust they would be in very good shape indeed. There was a major grievance that the All Black lock, Ali Williams, had got away unpunished with a blatant stamp on Josh Lewsey's head, leaving England's full-back with a nasty cut. But the team had to move on, in every sense. Having achieved only their second win in New Zealand in eight attempts (the previous one was in 1973), could England now add a first victory in Australia in 40 years and 10 defeats' worth of trying? Next stop, Melbourne.

A week after Wellington, England once more put their world ranking on the line. Again they faced opponents still fine-tuning their best line-up. Australia were missing a world-class flanker in George Smith, and a world-class fly-half in Steve Larkham. In the back three they were assimilating three ex-rugby league players in Wendell Sailor, Mat Rogers and Lote Tuqiri. Appreciation of rugby is wholly subjective, but with hindsight this was perhaps England's finest hour (and 20 minutes). The cutting edge they craved, and which had been mostly absent since the Six Nations campaign of 2001, returned with a vengeance. From the mobile front rowers, Trevor Woodman and Steve Thompson, to the flyers of the flanks, Lewsey, Jason Robinson and Ben Cohen, England took the game to their opponents. Johnson, the undisputed king of scrum, ruck and maul, showed some princely handling, too, and touched the ball four times in the 13-pass move that led to Will Greenwood's cracker of an opening try. Quick rucking and rapid support were essential. England were on song, and in tune with each other. They did not throw the ball around with abandon. They kept it and cherished it. Just after the half-hour, Mike Tindall ran in a second try made by forward pressure and sweet passes from Wilkinson and Greenwood.

Joe Roff potted a couple of penalties early in the second half, then Wilkinson knocked one over to make it 15–9 to England. A driving maul that rumbled the Wallabies back 50 metres was an extraordinary effort from England's pack. Cohen raced up the middle to a glorious third try, taking a pass from Wilkinson and easily outstripping the home full-back, Chris Latham. Towards the end Sailor stole a try, but Wilkinson boomed over a penalty goal to finish it off. It was England's fourth successive victory over the reigning world champions – the other three had been at Twickenham – and the Australian reporters were impressed. "Those in the southern hemisphere who have lampooned this England team for so long have to admit begrudgingly that this is a special side, capable of becoming the first nation from the north to raise the World Cup," wrote Greg Crowden in the Sydney *Sun-Herald*. In Melbourne's *The Age*, Ian Gilbert wrote: "This England side's secret is not the kicking machine in the No. 10 shirt [Wilkinson], but sheer, collective resolve."

England were buoyant as they flew west from Melbourne to Perth to check out their autumn accommodation. On the last day of June, the RFU management board announced that it was extending Woodward's contract through to the 2007 World Cup. "He has done an outstanding job for England and taken the side to new heights, on and off the field," said chairman Graeme Cattermole.

Making the Cut

By now England were on a winning run of 13 Tests spread over 18 months since a Six Nations Championship defeat away to France in March 2002. But Woodward was prepared to sacrifice a potential world record – 17 wins was the mark set by New Zealand in the 1960s and South Africa in the '90s – in order to fine-tune his World Cup selection. The warm-up squad comprised 43 players; outside this group was a 44th, Mike Catt, who followed a singular path into contention by undertaking "optimised conditioning", in the words of an RFU press release. Catt played for Bath in pre-season friendlies rather than engage in the Pennyhill Park grind. Apart from Catt, and Dallaglio and Vickery, who were resting minor injuries, each of the "definites", "probables" and "almost certainly won't be's" got a run at one time or another in the final three preparatory matches.

The first two were there to sort the wheat from the chaff. In Cardiff a shadow England XV won at a canter 43–9 against Wales' strongest side. There were tries for Lewis Moody, Dan Luger, Joe Worsley, Stuart Abbott and Dorian West – all five of whom would go to the World Cup. Indeed, seven of the starting pack went to Australia, and the eighth, Simon Shaw, eventually flew out as a replacement. The backs were not so fortunate. Four of the Cardiff selection would miss the cut.

Next England flew down to a stiflingly hot Màrseilles. A week of warm-weather training ended with another mix-and-match XV taking on a first-choice France in the 52,000-capacity Stade Vélodrome. England wore for the first time a tight-fitting, sweat-dispersing kit made by Nike. The French also wore a tight-fitting, sweat-dispersing kit made by Nike. The All Blacks, who had just completed their World Cup preparations by winning the Tri-Nations competition, did things differently – they wore a tight-fitting, sweat-dispersing kit made by Adidas.

Marseilles was buzzing; the French were up for the match, both crowd and team. England reprised the obduracy of their June tour by contesting every inch of ground – even a puff-chested Phil Larder obliged the brass band to march around him as he oversaw the players' pre-match drills. France were on top in the set-pieces of scrum and line-out, yet their danger men were mostly unable to escape the white blanket thrown over them by Larder's defence. England led 10–3 after a try by Tindall, who cut past his opposite number, Damien Traille. Then France's captain and scrum-half, Fabien Galthié, launched a counter-attack that made a try for full-back Nicolas Brusque. The stand-in for Wilkinson, Paul Grayson, had a close-up view of the lively young French sensation at No. 10, Frédéric Michalak. Here was a handful of a fly-half whom England would have to plan for if the two teams met again, as widely expected, in the semi-finals of the World Cup.

While Michalak was not as good as Wilkinson or Grayson in the goal-kicking department, he had a legitimate excuse for one miss when England's kitman, Dave Tennison, accidentally ran across his line of sight. With a meticulously-prepared team such as Woodward's, this was a grating faux pas. The coach apologised afterwards.

Ultimately, Michalak's three penalties and a dropped goal squeezed France home, 17–16, but against a virtual second-string England. Martin Corry and Iain Balshaw, offering power and panache fore and aft, did their World Cup chances no harm. The result itself soon faded from the forefront of pundits' minds, but it would stay crystal-clear in the thoughts of the French players, and might give England a psychological edge in the expected rematch in Sydney on 15 November.

For eight players September began with a kick in the teeth as Woodward announced the "initial cut" from the World Cup squad. For Steve Borthwick, Will Green, Andy Hazell, Jamie Noon, Alex Sanderson, Dan Scarbrough, Andy Titterrell and Dave Walder it was "Thanks a lot lads, better luck next time". A ninth man dropped out of contention two days before France emulated England and sent a reserve team out at Twickenham. Alex King, the Wasps fly-half who had been on the bench for the win over Australia in Melbourne, succumbed to a knee injury. Now the main talking points concerned the outside backs, the props and the second rows.

Cheered to the rafters by a capacity 75,000 crowd, England beat France comfortably, 45–14. A purple patch towards the end of the first half brought 21 points to transform the scoreline to 33–3. There were five tries, all scored by the outside backs including two for Cohen, who now had 23 in 29 Tests. Martin Johnson and Jonny Wilkinson were given short run-outs before being withdrawn early in the second half. Stuart Abbott limped off, but the South African-born centre already knew he had done enough. The situation surrounding another son of the Republic, Catt, was less clear.

The next day, a Sunday, Woodward revealed his hand. Catt was in; so too was Corry of Leicester, thanks to his ability to cover several positions in the pack. The final five to miss out were James Simpson-Daniel, Austin Healey, Graham Rowntree, Simon Shaw and Ollie Smith. "Not to pick Shaw or Rowntree are the two hardest decisions I've had to make in my six years as head coach," said Woodward, but the debate was over. There was a farewell dinner attended by 2,000 people in one of the car parks at Twickenham. Jonny Wilkinson was mobbed by autograph hunters and had to be smuggled out of the marquee by security guards. On Wednesday 1 October the squad said farewell to family and friends and posed for photographs on the steps leading up into Flight BA015 to Perth.

The final team briefing from Woodward before leaving Pennyhill Park was uplifting and devoid of the fear factor often associated with the country's failings in football and cricket. "Let's enjoy it," he said. "Let's not hide. Let's relish the pressure – there's no doubt we play better in that environment. I want to enjoy this, I want to win. And when we come back, and shake hands at the end of it, let there be no regrets. Let's say we gave it absolutely everything."

One of the coach's favourite terms was an acronym of "Thinking Correctly Under Pressure". After years of preparation, England were off down under to discover if the opponents ranged against them could whip up a storm to counter Woodward's T-CUP.

Lewis Moody, Mike Catt, Kyran
Bracken, Will Greenwood, Jonny
Wilkinson and Jason Robinson after
receiving their World Cup caps in Perth.

Lawrence Dallaglio lines up with team-mates Neil Back (left), Jonny Wilkinson and Mike Tindall before taking on New Zealand at the Westpac Stadium in Wellington.

Fly-half Carlos Spencer leads the
New Zealand Haka before the match
against England.

Left Martin Johnson gets away from Chris Jack of New Zealand during the Test match at Wellington.

Above Hooker Steve Thompson on the charge during England's 15–13 victory in the one-off Test against the All Blacks at the Westpac Stadium, Wellington.

Jonny Wilkinson kicks a penalty with the assistance of Mike Tindall during the Test match at Wellington.

Left Tana Umaga of New Zealand loses the ball under pressure from Lawrence Dallaglio and Martin Johnson.

Above Joe Worsley celebrates after the final whistle in Wellington. England won 15–13.

Left Mike Tindall is tackled by Joe Roff of Australia at the Telstra Dome in the Test at Melbourne.

Right Steve Thompson gets the better of Australia's Nathan Grey.

An England fan mocks Australian
supporters during the match at the
Telstra Dome in Melbourne.

Ben Cohen races in for a try as team-mate Jason Robinson starts to celebrate. The Australians are George Gregan (left) and Wendell Sailor.

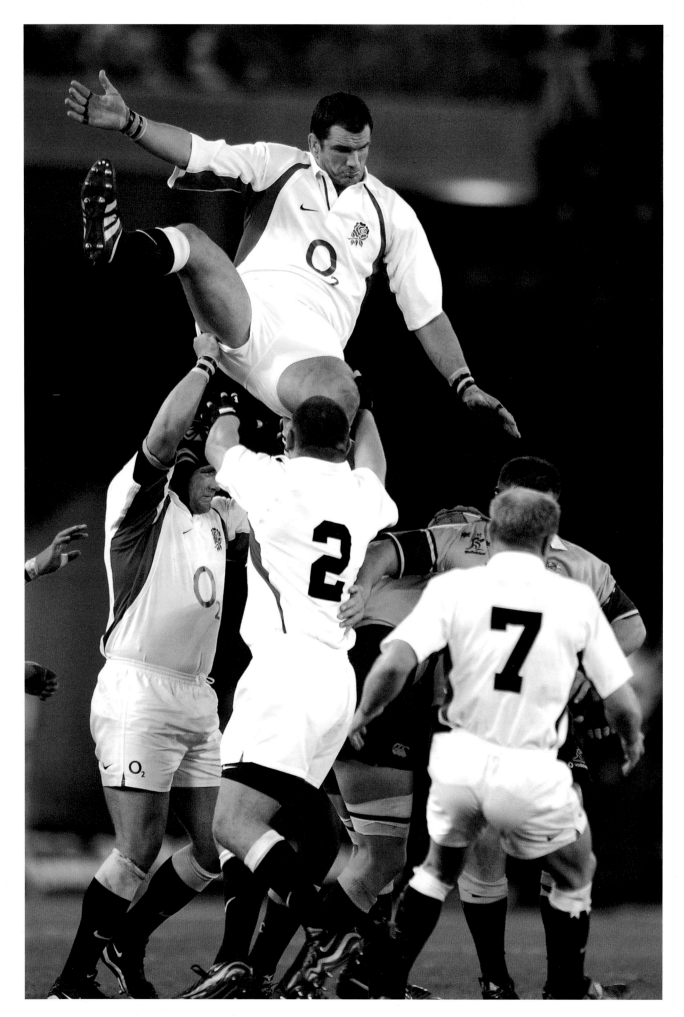

Opposite Martin Johnson is launched high during a line-out.

Left England captain Martin Johnson after his team defeated Australia to retain the Cook Cup. England won 25–14.

Below The victorious England team with the Cook Cup.

Left England players including Steve Thompson and Lawrence Dallaglio improve their reflexes by catching a tennis ball at a training session.

Above Ben Kay lifts weights at Pennyhill Park.

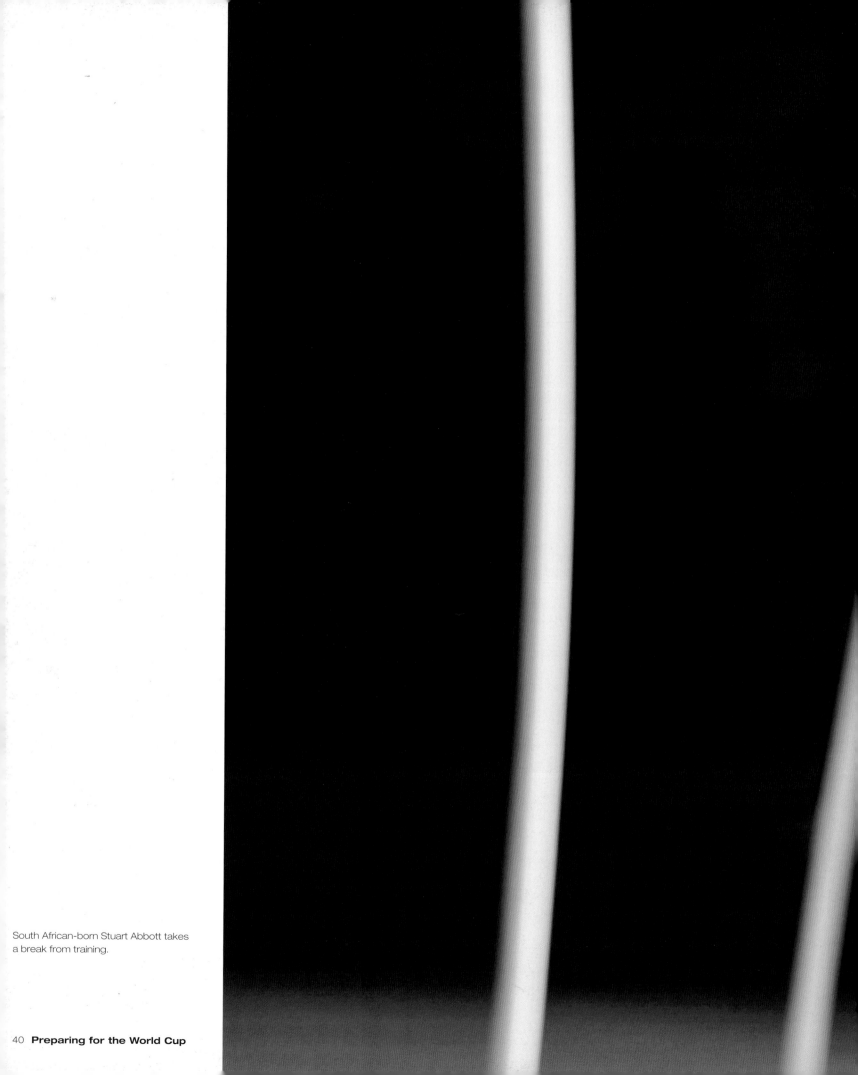

South African-born Stuart Abbott takes
a break from training.

Above A Welsh fan reacts as his team is soundly defeated by England at the Millennium Stadium in Cardiff. England won 43–9.

Right Stuart Abbott is caught by Robin McBryde of Wales.

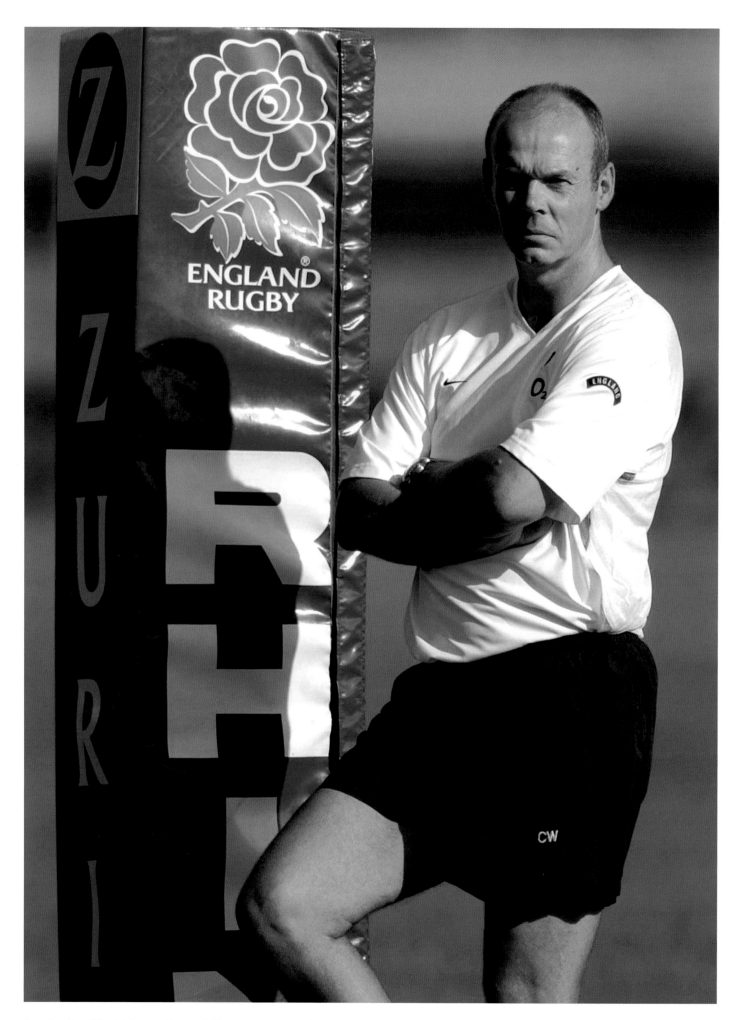

Left Clive Woodward watches training at Pennyhill Park.

Above Martin Corry (left) and Lewis Moody enjoy a game of table football at the Domain de Tournon Hotel in Aix-en-Provence, France.

Damien Traille holds on to Mike Tindall
in the France v England friendly at the
Stade Vélodrome, Marseilles.

Paul Grayson dejected as French players (left to right) Yannick Bru, Serge Betsen, Brian Liebenberg, Jérôme Thion and Olivier Magne enjoy their narrow win. France won 17–16.

Above Ben Cohen gets between Andy Gomarsall (left) and Jason Robinson.

Right Martin Johnson adjusts his headgear in training at Pennyhill Park.

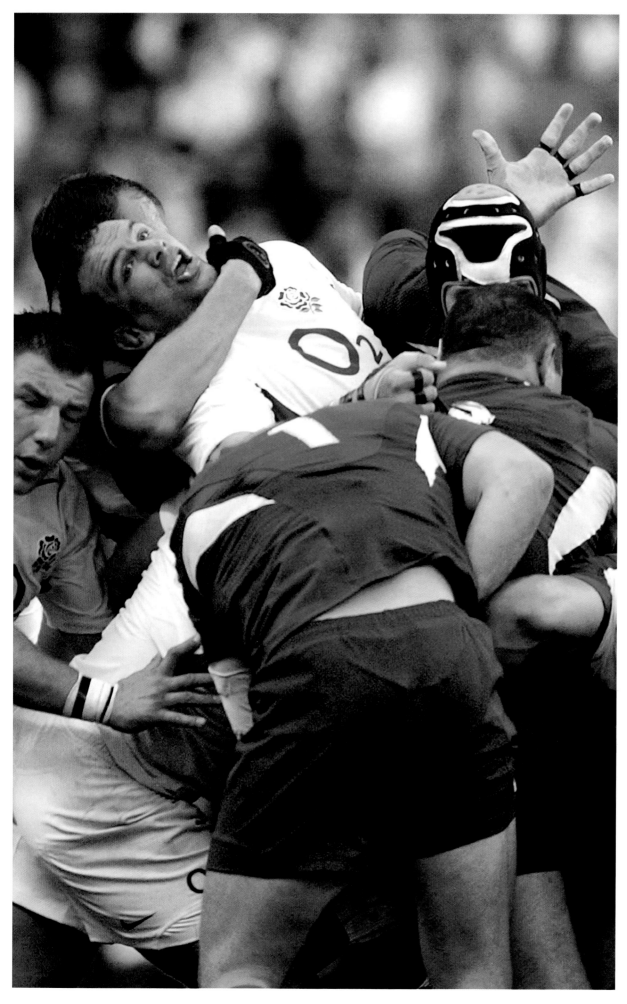

Previous pages Rainclouds threaten Twickenham during the final World Cup warm-up match against France. England won 45–14.

Above Steve Thompson tussles with Clément Poitrenaud (15) and Raphaël Ibañez at Twickenham.

Above Will Greenwood looks concerned as he gets a pass away to Jonny Wilkinson at Twickenham in the match against France.

Right Iain Balshaw keeps his eye on the ball as he is tackled.

Left All in a day's work for the captain, as Martin Johnson poses in a picture for Macmillan Nurses.

Right Jonny Wilkinson in matinee idol mood during a media day at the England training headquarters.

The World Cup: Pool Stage

The World Cup: Pool Stage

England made landfall in Perth, via Singapore, at one o'clock in the morning. Around 50 fans were there to greet them. The team checked into the Sheraton Hotel where the usual unpacking of kit was followed by a night of pacing around in an effort to nullify jetlag. The first few days allowed them the opportunity to relax, have a few beers and get their bearings. Soon enough, though, Dave Reddin had them working hard at Hale School, a well-heeled establishment on the edge of the city, 15 minutes' stroll from the Indian Ocean.

Woodward knew from experience that one opponent his men would have to take care of away from the field of play was the Australian press. In England, the team's success had made them popular with reporters, and press conferences – or media briefings, to use the parlance – tended to lack the confrontational fizz of their equivalents in soccer. They were less gladiatorial, with raised voices and hackles few and far between. On the occasions when football journalists were detailed to attend these events, they were uniformly taken aback by the lack of needle between Woodward and his inquisitors.

In Australia, the style is different. The writing in the press is more free-form and conversational than the coverage in British broadsheets. If Aussie journalists feel like criticising some aspect of a team's play, they will wade in, no holds barred. The truth is that usually they need not be taken too seriously. But the arrival of the good old Poms, who just happened to have a team to take seriously for a change, was bound to make for a combustible mix. The praise handed out by the Australian writers after the win in Melbourne was quickly forgotten. After England's first two pool matches in the World Cup, the supposed reliance for points on Wilkinson's boot prompted a splash headline on *The Australian*'s Monday sports supplement: "Is that all you've got?"

Normally, the Australian public would not give two hoots either way. Australian Rules football, better known as Aussie rules, and rugby league are much more popular than rugby union. But from the start the World Cup tournament was superbly organised and marketed, and crowds flocked to 10 grounds across the continent, including an extraordinary full house for Namibia v Romania in Launceston, Tasmania. Those new to it discovered that, leaving aside the apparent hostility of the press, rugby unites in a way football has too often forgotten. When England first played a Six Nations Championship match in Italy in 2000, the tale went that hundreds of Roman riot police were mobilised, only to be baffled by the sight of thousands of peaceable fans more likely to research the history of the Colosseum than tear the thing down. So it was in Australia. Taking their cue from the 20,000 supporters who followed the Lions' tour in 2001, around three times that number headed out from the British Isles to support England, Ireland, Scotland and Wales, and have a damned good party while they were at it.

By the time England reached Sydney for the business end of the tournament, the rugby version of cricket's Barmy Army was estimated at 45,000. Their favourite gathering point was down by Darling Harbour, a couple of drop kicks from the Opera House, and boasting a nice selection of watering holes. A typical supporter would be wearing a replica England jersey, usually of the non-skintight variety (and good business for the

Previous pages England head coach Clive Woodward watches a wet training session at Scotch College in Melbourne.

Above Jonny Wilkinson calls the shots during the Rugby World Cup Pool C match against South Africa at Subiaco Oval, in Perth, Australia.

manufacturers at up to £50 a throw), and be accompanied by members of the family or a couple of mates. If they found themselves sharing a bar with another nationality there would be an outbreak of singing, not fighting. True, their Aussie hosts could get a bit uppity, and did they really have to go on all the time about the bloody Pommies? Overall, though, the trip was worth the thousands of pounds laid out on the often exorbitantly priced official travel packages. Not least because most of the fans were convinced that England would advance to the semi-finals, if not go all the way.

Georgia

Rugby is surprisingly popular in Georgia, to the extent that crowds of 40,000 have been known for Test matches in the capital, Tbilisi – albeit when the bitter rivals from Russia are in town. But the Georgians' World Cup preparations were starkly different from England's: they were penniless, not Pennyhill Park. Billeted in an unprepossessing quarter of a seaside resort close to Montpellier in the south of France, the first-time qualifiers' team bonding for Australia was somewhat undermined by the fact that some of them didn't want to go. These players were on contracts with first and second division clubs in France, and they were being leant on by their employers to stay behind. Their wages, though modest by English standards, went a long way in the economically ravaged Caucasus. Three of the Georgians who bowed to French pressure and failed to turn up for the World Cup were later suspended from playing for their clubs by the French Federation – they were the only players against whom IRB regulations were invoked, even though there were withdrawals for similar reasons from the squads of Tonga, Samoa, Fiji and Canada. The IRB promised to address the problem, largely an economic one faced by impoverished unions, in time for 2007.

The Georgians' plight earned sympathy in Perth. Clancy's Fish Pub in Subiaco Village was set up as the official meeting place for the hastily formed Georgia Supporters' Club, and the University of Western Australia Rugby Club offered the team training facilities and local rugby contacts. The players who were keen to take part, even at a cost to themselves and their families, anticipated the opening Pool C fixture against England with a mixture of pride and trepidation. "Martin Johnson is a legend," said Viktor Dideboulidze, with a faraway look in his eyes that was somehow at odds with his menacing dimensions at 6ft 6in and 19 stones. Dideboulidze was one of only two men in the squad over the age of 30. In addition to the non-travelling recalcitrants, the other main absentee was Ilia Zedginidze, the captain and No. 8, who was recovering from a smashed cheekbone sustained in a warm-up match in Italy.

England, by contrast, were at full strength. They had made it through a tough summer without suffering a calamity like Zedginidze's, and Woodward had consistently promised to field his top line-up as the correct step along the World Cup pathway rather than any particular mark of respect for the opposition or the tournament. No one knew it at the time, but the XV who kicked off England's bid for the Webb Ellis Cup against Georgia in Perth on Saturday 12 October would be the same XV who contested the final in Sydney 41 days later. It was also the team who had

accounted for Australia in Melbourne the previous June, with the exception of Matt Dawson, who was not fully fit on the summer tour.

So the roll call against Georgia was a thoroughly familiar one – Josh Lewsey, Jason Robinson and Ben Cohen in the back three, Mike Tindall and Will Greenwood at centre, Matt Dawson and Jonny Wilkinson as half-backs. At forward, a pack of Trevor Woodman, Steve Thompson and Phil Vickery, Martin Johnson and Ben Kay, Richard Hill, Neil Back and Lawrence Dallaglio. The last three names had merged into one by now – "Hillbackdallaglio" – and tripped off the tongue like a sergeant's order: "ready-aim-fire". In a young man's game of fearful collisions and terrifying fitness levels, this was a trio of Canutes holding back time so that they could add to their world record 33 appearances together. There had been a couple of blips over the previous 12 months when both Back and Dallaglio were dropped at various times in favour of Leicester tyro Lewis Moody. In Perth the old guard were reunited for when it mattered most.

Georgia were no featherweights in the forwards but neither could they draw on the stock of technique or street wisdom available to England. It was a rout, and a wet one at that. England cantered to 12 tries in conditions made trickier by a six-hour downpour which swept in from somewhere spiteful over the Indian Ocean. Rain would follow Johnson and company across Australia. Dallaglio emphasised England's forward superiority with a pushover try – almost unheard of in international rugby – after 45 minutes. Tindall got the try-scoring going in the 15th minute, gliding through the Georgian cover after a long pass by Wilkinson, who had previously posted England's opening points of the tournament with a penalty goal. The Georgians tackled and tackled – 154 of them to England's 41 – but they trailed 34–3 at half-time, and it was 84–6 by the end. "We didn't let up for a second," said Andy Robinson, Woodward's assistant.

It was a satisfactory evening's work – or Sunday lunchtime's viewing and listening if you were back home. But the Australian observers got to work on any England weakness they could find, real or imaginary. John Eales, a wonderful player who captained the Wallabies to their World Cup win in 1999, hit upon the so-called "truck and trailer" method of certain players – usually Back or Dallaglio – carrying the ball behind a phalanx of fellow forwards without binding onto them as the law demanded. "It's certainly the equivalent of obstruction," rapped Eales, "and it's the equivalent of a decoy play in the backline." Which, even if the questionable charge was true, made it all right in the eyes of English supporters, who believed the Australian backs had been obstructing opponents with their own decoy moves for years.

South Africa

Team meetings are essential to the smooth running of operations, and can take various forms during the build-up to a match. A senior group of Woodward, Johnson, Dallaglio, Wilkinson and Greenwood might gather together to chew the fat; the forwards could have a pow-wow with Andy Robinson, and any particular unit of the team can spend their own quality time as they see fit. When the entire squad meet up it bears a passing resemblance to a school chemistry lab, with a coach or a player up front

A moment of ennui for Lawrence
Dallaglio in Melbourne.

gesturing at a white board full of mysterious markings, while the rest chew their pencils and make notes, at least of the bits they comprehend.

Most of what is discussed goes unreported in newspapers. There are two reasons for that: firstly, the team are not at all keen on having their plans and ploys revealed to opponents. And secondly, most of the reporters would have at best only a basic understanding of what was being talked about anyway. The long list of line-out calls and the thick playbook of different options used by the backs are nigh on impossible to convey with accuracy in a newspaper match report. Much easier not to try, and instead describe the effects, rather than the cause.

In a typical get-together, Wilkinson, as the backs' playmaker, might stand front and centre with his marker pen and issue instructions with codewords memorised by his colleagues like a cashpoint PIN number: "Jack", "Flash", "Nuts", "Killer", "Worm", "the split-miss". All simple stuff, if you happened to have trained with England for a couple of years. "The wolfie", intoned Wilkinson before the second pool match against South Africa. "Three-three split, missile early, getting at their 10, a poor defender on this side, split-miss, playing on that 13 channel, giving their 12 something to step into…" The team reserved a special call for when the plan was not entirely working and defence was of the essence: "Hit the Beach", which translated as "do whatever the hell is necessary to stop the opposition getting the ball".

At the end of the meetings, the players' notes were fed into a paper-shredder. England had already earned headlines in Perth for getting Tony Biscombe, the squad's video analyst, to sweep their hotel rooms for listening devices. It certainly gave a new meaning to the term "rugger bugger". The reports did not elaborate on how often the de-bugging took place. Was once a week enough? What happened if the spies from the bad guys got in the next day, to deposit their sinister mechanical agents?

The story was a good one to fill the papers alongside the routine tales of tweaked hamstrings and troublesome calf muscles. Yet an utterly genuine tale of human interest was brewing in the camp, one which cloaked the forthcoming contest against the South Africans with a shroud of pathos. Will Greenwood, the talkative muse of England's midfield and probably their most naturally creative player, harboured a secret known only to him and Woodward. A year before, Greenwood and his wife Caro had lost their son, Freddie, within an hour of the baby's premature birth. Now, Caro was experiencing complications with her second pregnancy, and Greenwood was torn between an immediate flight home and playing the South Africa match and then going. Later, he explained the dilemma: "[When you're] 12,000 miles away, [and] your wife is in intensive care, rugby training and the games were almost a break from the constant thinking." In seeking to do the right thing, Greenwood talked it over with Woodward, but kept the developing situation from his team-mates. As a naturally garrulous individual, he knew he could not expect the others to spark off him as he and they were used to if they were, however subconsciously, guarding against upsetting him. In the end, Greenwood played – but as he looked around the dressing-room at the Subiaco Oval in the moments before kick-off, only he of the 22 players knew that he was booked on a flight out of Perth two hours after the final whistle.

The style and grace of Jonny Wilkinson, kicking in the Pool C match against Samoa at the Telstra Dome in Melbourne.

Victory over South Africa was the key to England winning Pool C. The draw for the knockout stage had been made months previously, with the top team in the pool set to face the runners-up of Pool D, likely to be Wales. Losing to the Springboks would mean England meeting the winners of Pool D, almost certainly the All Blacks. "The pressure going into that [South Africa] game was more than any other ever," Woodward said later. "More than for the final, or for the semi-final. Everyone realised that if we won this game, this team would take off and we were going to win this damned thing." In the team meeting beforehand, he told his players: "I believe we're fitter and faster, if we play at the pace we know we can play at." The white board of instructions carried only one South African name: "VD Westhuizen". In full, Joost van der Westhuizen, the Springbok scrum-half, sole survivor of the Rainbow Nation's 1995 World Cup triumph. Indeed he was the sole survivor of the 18 Springboks who featured in the quarter-final against England at the '99 tournament. Van der Westhuizen, one of the game's all-time greats, was rated by Woodward as both South Africa's rallying point and their Achilles' heel. "Everyone's been talking about him," said the coach. "I think he's a weakness. We want to be all over him."

England had a problem of their own at scrum-half. Matt Dawson strained a knee against Georgia, and Kyran Bracken had pulled out shortly before kick-off with spasms in his back. World Cup rules stated that a new player could join the squad only if the man replaced dropped out for the duration. Neither Dawson nor Bracken had got to that stage, but Woodward did not want to be caught short a long way from home if they did. He had no hesitation in executing Plan B, which was to fly out a standby – Bath's Martyn Wood – who would then be kept at arm's length, forbidden by the rules from participating in training sessions or even entering the team hotel. Wood was having Sunday lunch in Bath when he got a call telling him to get to Heathrow for a flight to Perth in three hours' time. Forty-eight hours later he was on his way back to Bath, and indeed played for his club in a Premiership match the following weekend. Bracken needed to wear a corset to protect his back, but he was declared fit to face the Springboks. Wood said: "It wasn't like I was in quarantine, and I also had more sleep than I've ever had in my life. I would have loved to have been involved but it wasn't to be."

As with 44 of the 48 World Cup fixtures, the match was scheduled for an evening kick-off. There was a festival atmosphere at the Subiaco Oval. Flags of St George were plastered everywhere, with some of their owners in a similar state. Face-painting was all the rage for the kids – a fashion that had started with England's football followers at Euro '96 had crossed over into rugby. For months in Perth, there had been good-natured banter across garden fences over World Cup bragging rights: the thousands of ex-pat Britons living in the city are outnumbered only by the ex-pat South Africans.

England had humiliated the Springboks 53–3 at Twickenham the previous November in an ugly encounter that saw the lock, Jannes Labuschagne, sent off for a late tackle on Jonny Wilkinson. All sorts of off-the-ball misdemeanours were replayed on television and Corne Krige, the Boks' captain and one of the principal offenders, more or less promised revenge in Perth. In the last days before the match Woodward, fearing a

Andy Gomarsall plays basketball with six-year-old burns patient Miah Churchill during a visit to the Princess Margaret Hospital for Children in Perth, Australia.

bust-up before the first whistle, called for the teams to enter the pitch separately. It was not one of the coach's better ideas and the organisers sensibly denied the request.

The teams having resisted the temptation to tear into each other in the tunnel, the most eagerly awaited match of the World Cup so far kicked off, with almost 40,000 spectators in attendance. South Africa were lively, with the volatile Krige flanked in the back row by two quick youngsters, Juan Smith and Joe van Niekerk. An unfamiliar figure in the front row, Christo Bezuidenhout, helped maintain the Boks' proud reputation in that department with a strong performance against Phil Vickery. England were missing Richard Hill, who had strained a hamstring against Georgia. The press were told he would not be out for too long.

Greenwood's game was admirable in the circumstances, save for one unusual incident near the end of the first half. A penalty attempt had gone wide from Louis Koen, South Africa's fly-half, and ordinarily whoever collected the ball would ground it behind the posts and take a restart. Instead, Greenwood forgot to ground the ball and simply chucked it to a team-mate – in effect, a forward pass. The resulting scrum, with the Springboks on the attack, might have led to a hugely damaging setback just before the interval. But England escaped when Kyran Bracken cleverly stole possession back at a ruck.

Koen must already have suspected it was not to be his night. He was by no means the first goal-kicker to discover that Wilkinson is a tough act to emulate. England's No. 10 kicked his side into the lead after three minutes and added another penalty just before the half hour. Koen, by contrast, had a woeful time of it. He put a penalty over after 18 minutes – not long after a trademark Jason Robinson break almost made a try for Mike Tindall – but missed in the 22nd minute, the 32nd, the 35th and the 37th.

It was 6–6 at the interval, Koen having put over his second attempt in six just before the whistle, but it might have been much worse for England. Wilkinson was not prominent in the attacking phases and Hill's stand-in, Lewis Moody, conceded a couple of penalties through over-eagerness as much as anything malicious. Still, with Wilkinson continuing to hit the target with two penalties in the third quarter, England moved out to 12–6, and the Boks blew another chance when full-back Jaco van der Westhuyzen wasted a promising overlap. The pressure from England, with Ben Kay nicking the occasional line-out, and Neil Back scrapping ferociously on the deck, soon told. A dreadful low pass from van der Westhuizen was the red rag to Moody's bull and the flanker hounded Koen and charged down the attempted clearing kick with both arms. The ball squirted backwards towards the South African posts. Greenwood, ever alert to all possibilities, followed up. He ran 20 metres, hacked the ball on another 15, and dived on it for the only try of the match. Greenwood raised himself onto one knee and grinned broadly at the fans and photographers behind the goal. Mike Tindall rushed up behind, cheekily poking out his tongue, and the photo of the pair of them soon flashed around the world. It told a tale of England on top, but still only Greenwood on the field knew the full story behind his celebrations. Later, when the facts were known, Johnson said: "Will, playing that game – and the way he did – was phenomenal. I don't think I would have been able to do it."

The try, converted by Wilkinson to maintain his 100 per cent record, gave England breathing space at 19–6. A few minutes later, Wilkinson dropped a goal to increase the lead, while poor Koen was withdrawn, a sad figure, to be replaced by Derick Hougaard. England's fitness was holding up well, Wilkinson dropped another goal in the closing stages for good measure, and although the final 25–6 scoreline did not perhaps reflect all the facets of the match, it was an absolutely acceptable outcome against one of the traditional powerhouses of the southern hemisphere.

Samoa and Uruguay

While Greenwood made his week-long round trip home and back – Caro would deliver a healthy baby boy, Archie Frederick Lewis, at the end of January 2004 – England flew to Melbourne and set their sights on the final two matches in Pool C, against Samoa and Uruguay.

The Samoans were a tricky prospect. For one thing, several of their better known players had, like the Georgians, chosen not to take part. There were some unfamiliar names on the teamsheet, alongside the likes of Terry Fanolua and Earl Va'a, who had both enjoyed long spells with English clubs. Neither had Samoa's rumbustious performances in previous World Cups been forgotten. In 1991, 1995 and 1999 they had forged a formidable reputation for fierce tackling and plenty of skill, beating Wales twice in Wales, and reaching two quarter-finals.

Here, under the roof of the Telstra Dome, they reminded the world of their superb handling play. The try in the seventh minute, which went through 11 phases and was finished by captain Semo Sititi, was a classic of its kind. Months later it was carried on the IRB's website as the preamble to a live streaming of the draw for the 2007 World Cup. A wonderful moment, unless you happened to be English.

To win a World Cup, a team must adapt to every kind of challenge. England could not rely on Va'a to do a Louis Koen: the Samoan fly-half kicked three penalties in the first half as his side turned round an improbable 16–13 in front. Wilkinson, by contrast, missed for the first time in the tournament, albeit from long range in the 14th minute. It was, indeed, his first miss in 25 attempts since the June tour, and the feeling of surprise – shock, even – was intensified when he struck a post from a relatively easy position shortly before half-time. "In all fairness," said Mike Tindall afterwards, "when you're 10 points down and Wilko hits the post you think to yourself 'hmm, we could be in the shit here'." In between, Wilkinson converted a try when Neil Back was driven over from a line-out. Even so, without Richard Hill, England's back row of Back, Dallaglio and Joe Worsley were being shaded by Sititi, Peter Poulos and Maurie Fa'asavalu.

The second half offered no immediate respite for the favourites. A Wilkinson drop at goal went wide in the first attack, and Samoa through Va'a's punt swept back upfield. Stuart Abbott, making his World Cup debut for England, broke out of defence but spilled the ball in a tackle by Sititi. Though Martin Johnson was leading by example, England could not get the concerted phases going, and became bogged down exploring the narrow channels. Then Fanolua went off injured and a chink of light appeared in the Samoan defence. Referee Jonathan Kaplan awarded a penalty try when

Clive Woodward leaves an IRB hearing in Sydney on 30 October. The hearing was held over the "16th man" affair in the Samoa match – England had 16 players on the pitch for a short time.

Samoa pulled down a back-pedalling scrum, and Wilkinson converted for England's first lead of the match, 20–16. Va'a chipped over a penalty in reply, and, incredibly, another from the 22 after Samoa stole a line-out to re-take the lead at 22–20 going into the last quarter.

Wilkinson dropped a goal, and Jason Robinson made another twinkling incursion into opposition territory. In the 71st minute, England deployed a favourite tactic from a line-out. Wilkinson launched a crossfield kick, catching Samoa's wing Sailosi Tagicakibau upfield; Iain Balshaw glided in for the try. Mike Catt came on for Abbott – one South African-born centre for another – and England got another try through a bullocking run by Vickery who, like Steve Thompson, had started on the bench and celebrated his score with a passion which said everything about the way the match had panned out. Wilkinson's conversion gave him 15 points to 17 by Va'a. Samoa had won the day too, gloriously so, in the romantic and attacking senses. But the ultimate victory was England's, 35–22.

Catt later observed that previous England teams might have buckled in the same situation. "This team never got rattled," he said. "It's a sign of a team that's been together for so long – they understand what needs to be done. You talk about the Lawrence Dallaglios and the Neil Backs, and these are the blokes who will be standing next to you at the gates of Hell. And you don't have to ask for their help; they'll give it, gladly. That goes for everybody in the squad."

What nobody in the squad was prepared for was the disciplinary storm about to break over England's heads – nobody that is except Woodward, who with almost clairvoyant prescience had added a QC, Richard Smith, to his backroom staff.

The problem occurred in the last few minutes of the Samoan match. Mike Tindall had been on the far side of the field from the coaches' seats, struggling to continue after a bang on the leg. Woodward, looking down from his glass-fronted eyrie, wanted Dan Luger on as a replacement and urgently sent the instructions down via his radio link to Dave Reddin. What followed was both fraught and confused. Tindall re-entered the field of play on one touchline, while Luger entered on the other. England under Woodward had sometimes been castigated for playing 10-man rugby. At other times, they were praised for an expansive 15-man game. Now, for all of 34 seconds, they had a go with 16 men. Afterwards, Reddin got into a spat in the tunnel with the No. 4 official Steve Walsh from New Zealand – the reserve for the referee and two touch judges. Some water was thrown, and insults, too. The Samoans made no protest, but in certain quarters – no prizes for guessing that the Aussie press soon got to work – England were accused of crimes ranging from a daft cock-up to downright cheating, with the old favourite of arrogance somewhere in the mix.

The World Cup organisers convened a disciplinary hearing in Sydney. If found guilty of wilfully breaking the rules, England were facing anything from a rap on the knuckles to losing points and their hard-earned leadership of the pool. "At the time it seemed the logical thing to do," said Woodward later of his instructions to Reddin. "It was the wrong call by me. What was the right call was having the QC down there. I've never been so nervous in my life." In a courtroom atmosphere in Sydney, Woodward's heart skipped a beat as the prosecution and defence said their pieces. Walsh was banned from World Cup duty for three days and had to stand down from running touch for France against the USA. England admitted their offence and received a £10,000 fine. Phil Kearns, the Wallaby captain turned pitchside commentator, was dismissive of the sentence: "England spend 10 grand on tea and biccies every afternoon." A relieved Woodward admitted: "I learnt a huge lesson that day. Richard Smith was fantastic."

In the meantime, the players were enjoying the many pleasures of Queensland's Gold Coast, where they were given four days off before the Uruguay match. They played golf, messed around at the Wet'n'Wild water park, had nights out and behaved almost like tourists. Even the "one game at a time" mantra could not disguise the truth that Uruguay in Brisbane would be less troublesome than Samoa in Melbourne.

There was still no Hill, about whom the medical bulletins became less illuminating as they grew more numerous. But England were expected to win by a wide margin, and duly did so. Though they were not thoroughly fluent in their play, they had significant and predictable advantages in power, pace and co-ordination. Combined, they gave England their highest win in a World Cup match, 111–13. Josh Lewsey, a veteran of the awful 1998 tour who had spent some of the interim in the Army, route-marched his way to five of the 17 tries, equalling the individual England record held by Rory Underwood and Douglas Lambert. Reserve scrum-half Andy Gomarsall enjoyed himself, darting this way and that with a wide variety of passes to maintain the flow of tries. Mike Catt, the late call-up to the squad, proved his fitness and sharpness. Martin Johnson and Jason Robinson were brought on from the bench a few minutes into the second half for a pre-planned loosener seven days before the quarter-final. The only low note concerned Joe Worsley, who had become a favourite of the media for his ability to knock out a tune on the piano at the drop of a tuning fork. Worsley was sent to the sin bin for a high tackle on the Uruguayan wing, Joaquin Pastore. As he walked off, he was applauded by some of the English supporters in the Suncorp Stadium, and responded in kind. Misguided? Certainly. Arrogant? Of course, in the opinion of England's detractors. "A huge error," Woodward called it. In fact, it turned out to be England's only yellow card of the tournament, an indication of the team's discipline under Johnson.

Without the need for much motivation, Woodward had used the team meeting before the Uruguay win to sum up England's progress to date. "We're exactly where we wanted to be," he said. "Played three, won three. I believe it's just [a case of] tweaking one or two things, no more than that. We're looking forward to a change of atmosphere from Melbourne to Brisbane." One thing he did not anticipate was the feeling of alarm on the bus back to the hotel, as the team listened to commentary on the last Pool D fixture, New Zealand against Wales. The Welsh, apparently more by luck than judgement, hit upon a try-scoring formula and gave the All Blacks a real hurry-up. It looked for a while as if England's efforts at winning Pool C had been mis-spent, and that instead of avoiding New Zealand in the quarter-finals they would be meeting them in less than a week's time. But the Kiwis recovered their poise to see off Wales by eight tries to four, and the anticipated Anglo-Welsh set-to, also to be played in Brisbane, was still on.

A fan watches in the rain as England take on Georgia at Subiaco Oval in Perth.

Left Dan Luger and Danny Grewcock were two of the lucky players to make the final squad of 30 for Australia.

Right England players settle into their first Australian training base at Hale School in Perth.

Below Martin Johnson (left) and Lawrence Dallaglio warm up.

Above The England team pose with a
giant rugby ball sand-sculpture at the
O₂ Beach Party on North Cottesloe
Beach, Perth.

Right King of the castle, England
flanker Neil Back.

Left Dorian West, who vied with Mark Regan to be back-up hooker to Steve Thompson, practises line-out throwing at Hale School.

Right Martin Johnson pushes a post in training at Hale School.

Left Matt Dawson on his way to a try against Georgia.

Right Josh Lewsey collides with Malkhaz Urjukashvili of Georgia in the Pool C match.

Left Ben Cohen kicked off with two tries against the Georgians.

Below Jason Robinson scores one of England's 12 tries in their opening World Cup match against Georgia.

Right Mike Tindall is tackled by two defenders during the match in Perth.

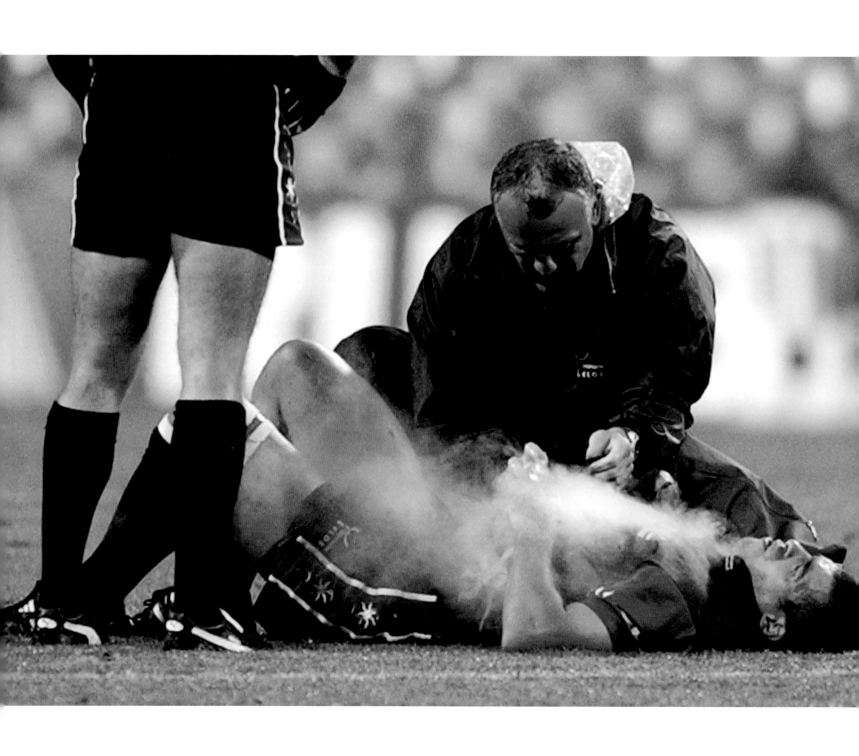

Georgian fly-half Paliko Jimsheladze is
treated after injury by team doctor
Jean-Louis Salomon.

Martin Johnson and Lawrence Dallaglio applaud the Georgia players off the field at the end of the match.

Left Mike Catt having a laugh during a training session at Hale School, Perth, watched by hundreds of schoolchildren.

Above High-stepping Stuart Abbott, Jonny Wilkinson and Trevor Woodman.

Above A cameraman in a helicopter films England in training at Hale School.

Right Clive Woodward looks skyward as a helicopter hovers overhead during an England training session. Woodward tightened security afterwards, even to the extent of sweeping hotel rooms for listening devices.

Left A South African fan cheers his team on to the field for the Pool C match against England.

Right Jason Robinson found it tough to get away from the South African tacklers.

Above Mike Tindall stretches in vain for the tryline before being bundled into touch against the Springboks.

Right South African lock Victor Matfield (left) grabs the ball while England centre Mike Tindall (second right) and Springbok captain Corne Krige take evasive action.

Above A bloody rematch of a previous encounter at Twickenham as Neil Back leaves the field with team doctor Simon Kemp.

Right England might have been behind at half-time had South Africa fly-half Louis Koen kicked better – Jonny Wilkinson shows Koen how it's done, early in the second half.

Martin Johnson looks to pass the ball as
South Africa's Joe van Niekerk moves in
for the tackle.

Left Not much is left of Johnson's skintight jersey, but England are on course for a crucial victory over the Boks.

Above Will Greenwood scores the winning try against South Africa.

Right Greenwood's celebrations masked a private ordeal for "the muse of England's midfield".

Martin Johnson gets his message
across during a training session in
heavy rain at Scotch College in
Melbourne.

Steve Thompson spins a pass out in a downpour during training.

Samoa lay down the challenge to England before their Pool C match at the Telstra Dome in Melbourne.

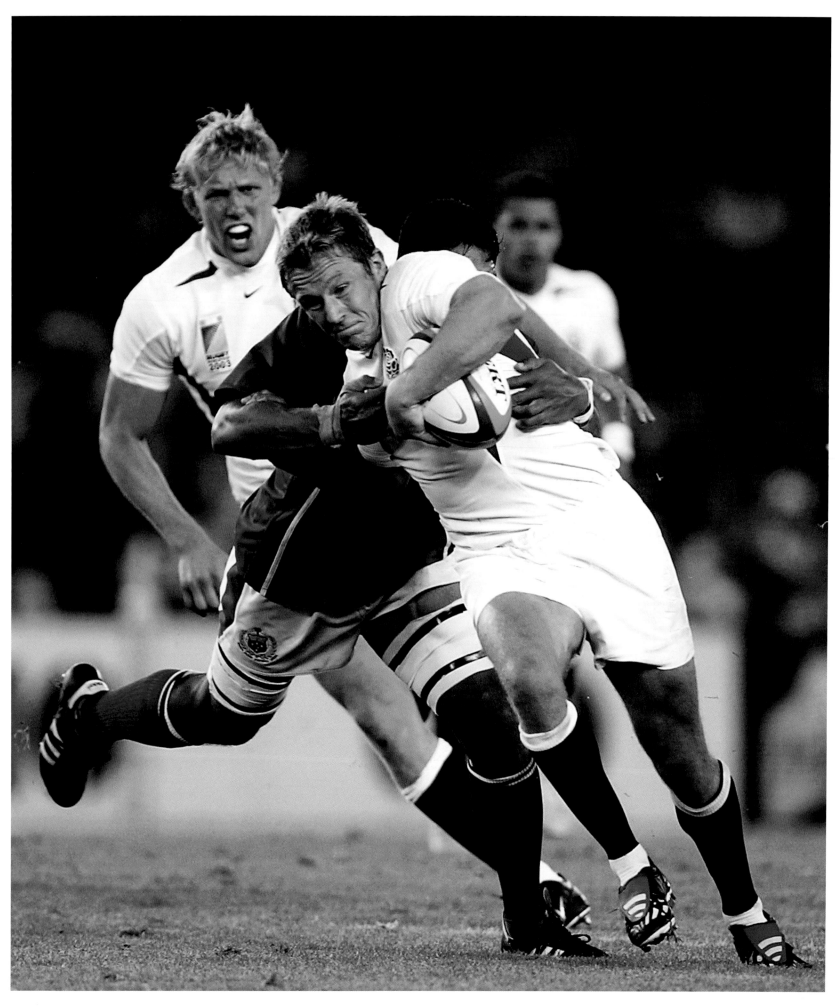

Left Jonny Wilkinson tries to get through a tackle against Samoa.

Above Stuart Abbott (left) and Mike Tindall combine to wrap up Samoa's Lome Fa'atau.

Above Neil Back scores a try and is congratulated by Lawrence Dallaglio. England scored four tries.

Right Jonny Wilkinson attempts a penalty goal against Samoa. He was not at his best with his place kicks.

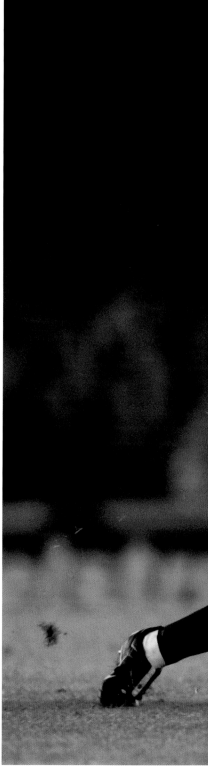

Above Phil Vickery elated after scoring
the try that sank Samoa.

Right Lawrence Dallaglio concentrates
on stopping a Samoa attack.

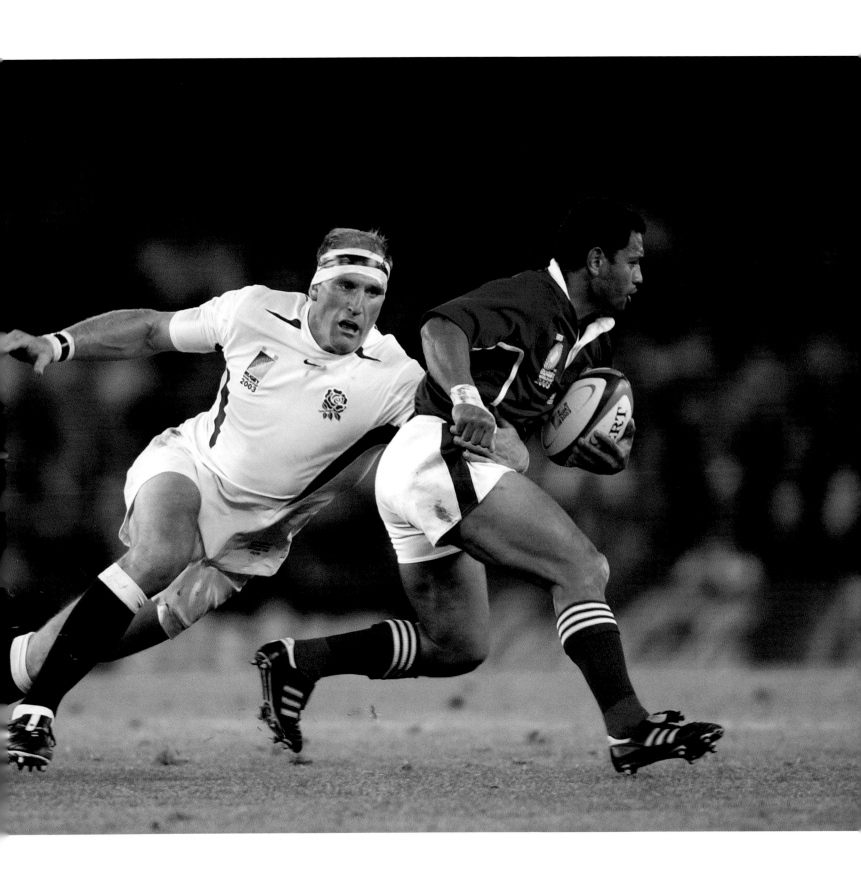

Above Matt Dawson and Ben Kay slide down a ride at Wet 'n' Wild on the Gold Coast in Queensland.

Left Lewis Moody comes down the "Twister" ride.

Right Matt Dawson and Ben Kay slide a ride.

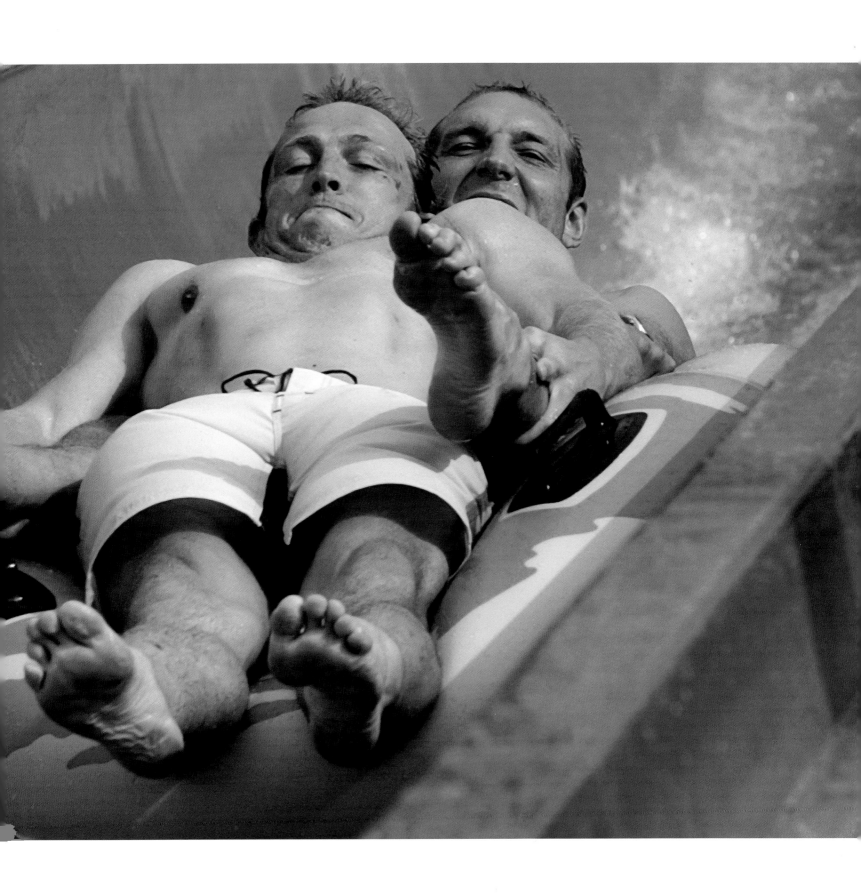

Ben Cohen relaxes during training at
Carrara Oval on the Gold Coast.

Left Matt Dawson, Mike Catt, Jason Robinson and Will Greenwood clown around.

Below left Ben Kay at Carrara Oval.

Below Martin Corry protects himself from the Gold Coast sun.

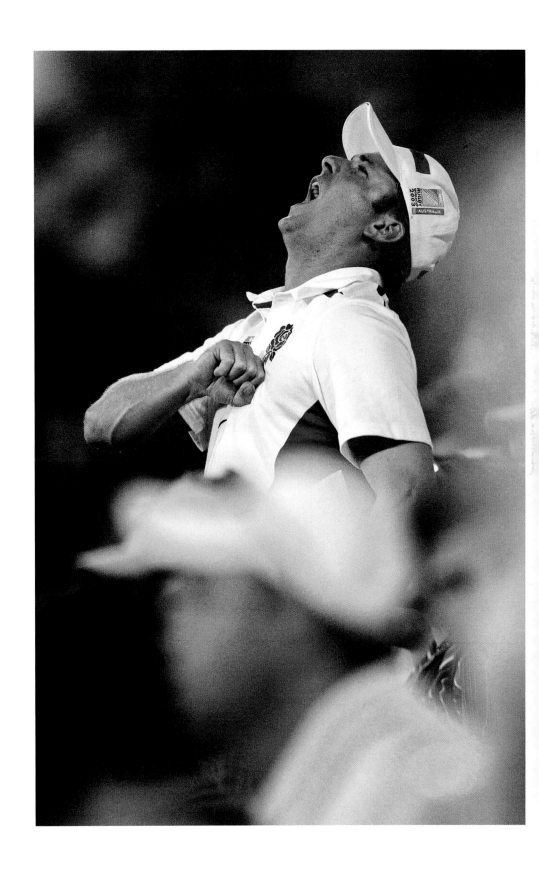

Left Uruguay fan Martin Demor cheers as his team enter the Suncorp Stadium in Brisbane. Uruguay were massive underdogs.

Right An England fan sings the national anthem before the Pool C match against Uruguay.

Lewis Moody scores England's first try against Uruguay – the first of 17.

Left Phil Vickery is stopped by the Uruguay pack.

Above Jason Leonard slips past Uruguay's fly-half Sebastian Aguirre.

Mike Catt makes a break. Catt celebrated his first start of the World Cup against Uruguay by scoring two tries.

Left A determined Josh Lewsey races downfield against Uruguay in Brisbane. He equalled the England record of five tries in one match.

Right Scrum-half Andy Gomarsall scores a try ahead of Sebastian Aguirre. The final score was 111–13 to England.

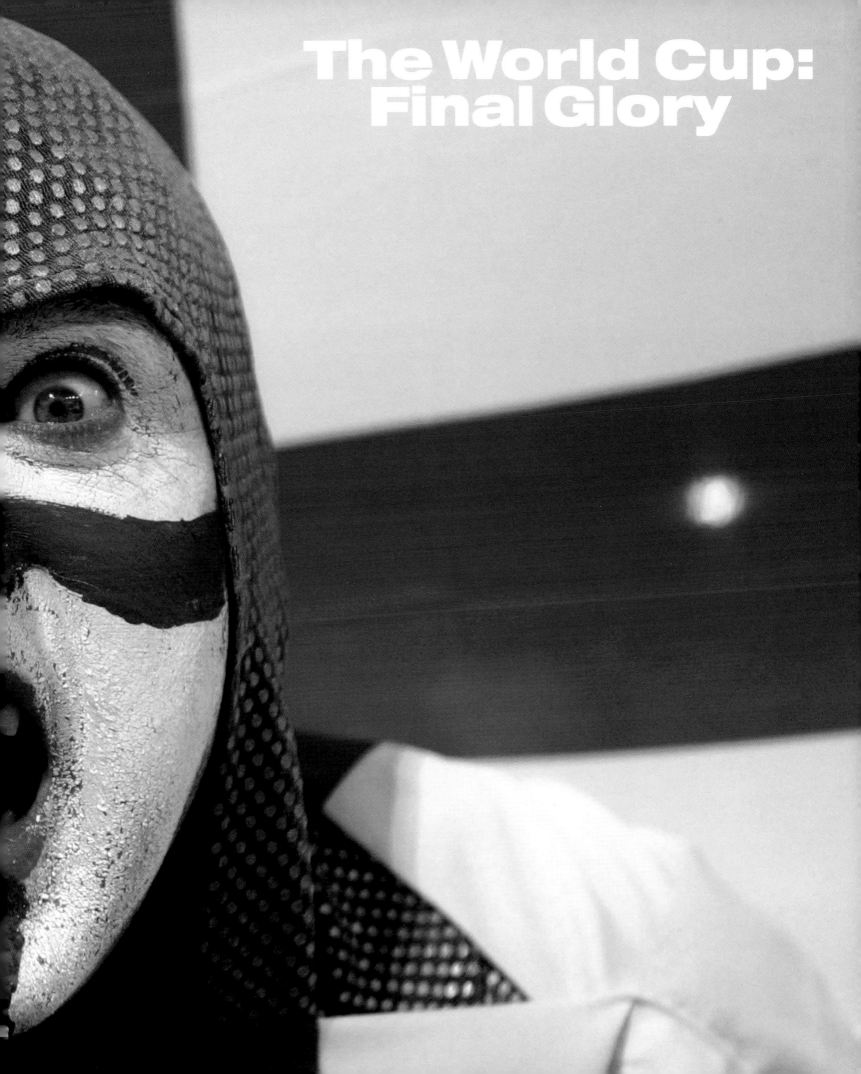

The World Cup:
Final Glory

The World Cup: Final Glory

After England's convincing win in Cardiff in the World Cup warm-up, one newspaper writer described the Welsh team as "confused, shapeless, spineless, deeply unprofessional and almost entirely skill-free". Things had changed. More or less out of the blue, Steve Hansen, Wales's New Zealander coach, stumbled on a way of playing which not only rattled the All Blacks but stayed true to the almost mythical sense of how the rugby-loving folk of the Principality like the game to be played. Put simply: "Run it from anywhere, boys!"

The game plan was made flesh in the slight frame of Shane Williams, a wing of great speed and intuition but, to Hansen, no more than a third-choice scrum-half when Wales arrived at the World Cup. A month into the tournament, Williams was magically an automatic choice in his favourite position. With two young chargers in the back row – Dafydd Jones and Jonathan Thomas – Wales suddenly had hope of a first win over the old enemy since the famous occasion at Wembley in 1999.

England checked out of their HQ on the Gold Coast and moved up to Brisbane, the city in which they had lost to Wales in the quarter-finals of the 1987 World Cup. That had been an abject match; this time around few expected either the quality of rugby or the result to be the same. England's principal worry was the number of penalties they had been giving away. A call of "Dead", when a questionable bit of possession had to be left alone, was deployed to guard against over-eagerness. Another bumper crowd filled the Suncorp Stadium, bringing together Leicester and Llandovery, Bath and Builth Wells, Coventry and Caernarfon. On the bench for England was a new face: Simon Shaw, the giant second row forward from Wasps, had flown in as the 31st member of the playing squad after Danny Grewcock broke a bone in his hand.

Jonny Wilkinson kicked a penalty to put England in front but two moments of poor decision-making betrayed his side's nerves. After 25 minutes Wales conceded a penalty within range of the posts, but instead of allowing Wilkinson to make it 6–0, Ben Cohen intervened and kicked across to the smallest forward on the pitch, Neil Back. It was the wrong option, it smacked of over-confidence and it came to nothing. Four minutes later, another poor kick was fielded by Shane Williams close to the Wales 22. The little man took one look at Ben Kay, and ran straight round him. He could probably have done two circuits of the hulking Leicester lock. This was Wales's Bruce Springsteen moment: born to run. Gareth Cooper hurtled across halfway and Stephen Jones, on the scrum-half's shoulder, finished off a thrilling try. Wales led 5–3.

England were rattled. "They're running through us like we're the Under-10s," muttered Woodward. Another Welsh raid on the England 22 ended with Dan Luger squirting a dreadful kick sideways into touch. Hoots of derision poured down from the ranks of red jerseys in the stands. It would be difficult to imagine a happier Welshman than one enjoying the discomfiture of the English. At least we're solid at the line-out, England told themselves. Wrong. Five minutes after the first try, a second for Wales, driven through England's line-out and scored by the captain, Colin Charvis. The half-time whistle came like the all-clear siren after a bombing raid. "If we'd gone 6–0 up," said Andy Robinson later, "I think we would have gone

Previous pages England fan dressed as a knight ready for quarter-final match against Wales in Brisbane.

Right Prince Harry and Jayne Woodward, wife of the England coach, celebrate after England defeat Wales at the Suncorp Stadium in Brisbane.

from strength to strength. Instead it turned around, and for the first time in the tournament in that 10-minute period we were on the ropes. We needed half-time to take the impetus out of the Welsh pack." Trailing 10–3, England headed down the tunnel with the Welsh fans playfully taunting Will Greenwood as the lookalike of the character from *Only Fools and Horses*: "How's that, Rodney Trotter?" The normally good-humoured Greenwood, who answers faithfully to the nickname "Shaggy", struggled to raise a grin.

Johnson was at his most vocal in the changing rooms. Matt Dawson had his say. Both of them had lost a World Cup quarter-final in 1999 and had no intention of making it a double. While his senior players gave the verbal hurry-up, added to by Phil Larder, Woodward acted decisively and substituted the out-of-sorts Luger with Mike Catt. The latter had only 90 minutes of Test rugby under his belt since November 2001, and had needed a hospital visit only a few days before this match after hurting his neck in training. Asked now to provide a spark, Catt did not disappoint. He took the pressure off Wilkinson with long passes and raking kicks to move the Welsh around and starve them of the ball.

Still, England needed a thrust of their own. Jason Robinson provided it, bursting between Mark Taylor and Gethin Jenkins on the Wales 10-metre line to make a try for the ever-ready Greenwood at the right-hand corner. Taylor almost toppled over as his opponent swept past him. That's what Robinson, aka Billy Whizz, does to people. A born-again Christian with dancing feet and a complex background rooted in a tough upbringing in Leeds, he was recruited by Woodward from rugby league in 2001. "I just try to find space," Robinson would say. "And if I don't know where I'm going, the opposition team is certainly not going to know."

England turned the screw. They let in Martyn Williams for a third Wales try, but steadily Wilkinson piled up 23 points from six penalties, a drop goal and the conversion of Greenwood's try. Not for the first time, England achieved the statistically rare feat of winning a Test despite being outscored on tries. The result was 28–17. "We were glad to get off the field," admitted Johnson, and the coaches, in the post-match debrief, did not spare the rod. Dallaglio was accused by Andy Robinson of "walking" and the team were shown on video replay how they were bunching together in one area of the field and therefore "playing narrow". It was crucial to England that the play was stretched wider, through several phases if necessary, to open the gaps up for Robinson and friends.

Woodward struck a balance by warning against an over-reaction to the performance. He repeated his belief that England would win the World Cup. He also stood up for the player unsurprisingly coming in for most public attention – Wilkinson. From rugby writers to columnists to psychiatrists, everyone had an opinion on the fly-half, and even if they didn't, they were invited to give one. So-called experts who wouldn't have known a kicking tee from a cup of tea believed they had identified deep-seated flaws in a 24-year-old who, in truth, gave every impression of being as straightforward a character as you could wish to meet. The fact that Wilkinson liked to strum a guitar in his room to unwind was improbably taken as an early sign of madness. Woodward left the amateur psychology to the pundits. He told his squad: "If he [Wilkinson] hadn't played, we'd have

Above Jonny Wilkinson training at the Telstra Stadium in preparation for the semi-final against France.

Overleaf England arrive at the Telstra Stadium in Sydney before their semi-final match with France.

lost this game. He's the world's best player, so who is anyone, including me, to say he's doing it wrong?"

As the dust settled on a nerve-tingling match, and Wales flew home to a quite unexpected heroes' welcome, England took stock. Woodward had expected Brisbane to be a welcome change from Melbourne, but the senior players felt like adapting the last words of George V, "Bugger Brisbane". They felt they had trained too hard in the Queensland heat. Woodward listened, and his coaches eased off the pedal. At the same time, they were inwardly delighted that almost the whole squad were fit and firing, so clearly Dave Reddin and his colleagues were doing something right. Richard Hill, a crucial cog in England's machine, who at a pinch might have faced the Welsh, would be fit for the semi-final. England, en masse, were ready for France.

The Semi-final

The day after eliminating Wales, the squad took what they knew would be the last of their internal flights, to Sydney, and checked into the Manly Pacific Hotel. The second man to be called from the UK on standby, Austin Healey, arrived and, like Martyn Wood before him, observed the ban on fraternising with the team. Over at France's HQ, the darlings of the World Cup media were bonhomie personified. Frédéric Michalak, a fly-half two years younger than Wilkinson, capably handled the abundant requests for interviews, showing off the diamond studs he wore in each ear. France had sailed through Pool B, easily defeating their principal rivals, Scotland, before dismissing Ireland emphatically in the quarter-finals. After the latter match, Fabien Galthié, France's captain and key player, embraced his Ireland counterpart, Keith Wood. Both men were retiring from rugby after the World Cup.

Galthié's outward warmth masked the fact that, privately, he was a worrier. Although a highly accomplished scrum-half, competing in his fourth World Cup, he worked himself into a lather about the weather. The day before the match, Galthié checked the forecast again and again. Rain was predicted, and he feared the English in the wet. Perhaps his anxiety communicated itself to the rest of the French team. Some people, including hooker Raphaël Ibañez, thought that, when the time came, they panicked. Not much, but enough.

England eyed the skies without suspicion as they downed their porridge in the breakfast room overlooking Manly Beach. They left for the Telstra Stadium – venue for the four matches remaining to complete the World Cup, including the dreaded play-off for third place – with dozens of fans forming a guard of honour in the lobby. "Come on England", went a shrill voice. The backs smiled, the forwards were stony-faced. Plus ça change. The windscreen wipers on the bus swished to and fro on the hour's journey west to Homebush in the city suburbs. Perhaps their motion matched the churning in Galthié's stomach. Was the Napoleonic figure in the blue No. 9 jersey looking for an excuse before the fact? After all, as Woodward said: "It rains in France, too, you know."

Catt played from the start for England. The French team were missing their anchorman and talisman in the pack, Pieter de Villiers, who had injured

himself falling off a mountain bike in pre-World Cup training. Otherwise the usual suspects were present and correct: Serge Betsen, Olivier Magne and Imanol Harinordoquy, who between them had fashioned a classic try against the Scots, were rated by many as highly as England's back row, even with Hill restored. But Andy Robinson did not believe the French trio defended anything like as proficiently as they attacked. England fancied they could make gains at the expense of the French scrum. As for their opponents' defence, which tended to be slung across the middle half of the pitch, England would either go wide and around it, or drive forward in numbers, then probe the short side as a launching-pad for further waves of attack. The game plan, needless to say, played to English strengths, while preying on a perceived French weakness – an inability in wet conditions to stem the flow without conceding penalties.

It worked. Within 22 minutes, France were down to 14 men, after a trip on Jason Robinson by Christophe Dominici that brought the Stade Français wing a yellow card. Dominici was the hero of France's advance to the 1999 final; here he injured himself making a ludicrous challenge and did not return from his 10 minutes in the sin-bin. For England, Hill ranged around the field as if he had never been away. Dallaglio, maintaining his record of playing every minute of every match, was in the faces of the French: challenging, tussling, grafting. Matt Dawson said: "I could see France thinking 'you should be attacking in the middle where all our players are'. Did they seriously think we were going to pitch up for a World Cup semi-final with nothing new up our sleeve?"

The front row did Andy Robinson's bidding and kept their opponents on the back foot, giving Michalak such a nightmarish mish-mash of possession that his influence was negligible and he eventually gave way to Gérald Merceron. As England attacked insistently and intelligently, France folded. Penalties were one consequence and Wilkinson went to work with the boot. The so-called "basket case" was back on song. By half-time, England led 12–7. There were two penalty goals from Wilkinson and dropped goals in the ninth and 39th minutes. "Sticking the knife in", Johnson called it.

There had been the blip of another try conceded by England at a line-out, but the scorer, Betsen, became the second Frenchman into the sin-bin when he late-tackled Wilkinson 11 minutes into the second half. Betsen hung his head as he departed (he was later accused of kicking Dawson at a ruck) and it soon became apparent the rest of his side were itching to get off the field with him. It must have been particularly satisfying for Wilkinson to see the downfall of Betsen; the Englishman had been hounded, bloodied and ultimately substituted in a previous confrontation with the French flanker in Paris in 2002.

"With 15 minutes to go," said Johnson, "we knew they weren't coming back." At the final whistle, Galthié, who would probably not feature in the third-place match and so had played his last, declined to swap jerseys with Dawson. Never mind. England, emphatic 24–7 winners, were in the World Cup final and in party mood. Jason Leonard's world record 112th cap was the trigger. A shirt with the number "112" was presented to the venerable prop, along with a ball from the semi-final stamped "SF03". Other England teams might have viewed reaching a final as an excuse to switch off and lose focus. Not this lot. Woodward set the stage for the biggest seven days of his players' lives, leading to the final the following Saturday evening. "As from tomorrow morning, expect chaos," said the coach. "It is absolutely critical to put everything on hold for one week. No distractions. Be stronger, more bloody-minded, piss the press off, agents, family, friends. The key word is 'No'."

The Final

Staying in Manly, England were hardly cut off from the world. They needed only to glance out of the window at any given moment to see people milling around, looking for autographs or photos. Notwithstanding Woodward's words, the players were treated as adults, and allowed to relax with their wives and girlfriends. Woodward himself was excited and relishing the sensations. He had lived, worked and played rugby in Sydney, so to return here with his masterplan for capturing the World Cup was a source of personal pride and joy. To announce an England XV to take part in the final was a thrill in itself. There was still the task of telling eight men that they would not be required, and a further seven that they would start the match on the replacements' bench. It went with the territory.

The forward pack picked themselves, after the way they performed against France. In the backs, the main bone of contention once again surrounded Catt, who was left out in favour of a recall for Tindall. Woodward was pleased with Catt's reaction. England were too close now – to each other spiritually, and to taking the cup – to worry that an individual player might throw a tantrum. The team room was plastered with posters pronouncing: "World class performance". The players behaved in kind.

England went into the final almost taken aback at their relaxed state of mind. The confidence stemmed from a deeply held belief that everything that could have been done, had been done. With the precise intention of reaching this moment, Woodward had prised several million pounds from the normally unyielding coffers of Twickenham. Only 80 minutes, and the reigning world champions, Australia, now stood between them and the game's ultimate prize. More than 80 minutes, as it would turn out...

Few of the locals had expected their own team to get this far. Australia had emerged top of a pool containing Ireland and Argentina, and defeated Scotland in the last eight. The day before England beat France, they upped the ante by knocking out the pre-tournament favourites, the New Zealand All Blacks, with a semi-final performance of astonishing intensity. The sheer bloody-mindedness of the Wallabies was now a significant factor in the story. Combined with nerves, loss of form or some other factor, it might yet scupper England's dreams.

The England team woke that Saturday morning to another grey Sydney sky, pregnant with rain. Each man was steeled to accept that the countless hours of training, the tedious pumping of weights and the tactical talks might all count for nothing in the face of something indefinable and unforeseen. In his final team meeting, Woodward quietly urged England to give of their best. "Nothing – nothing – will be left behind. Let's finish the job, get the f*** out of here and go home." On the way to the Telstra Stadium, the England bus passed Australians giving cheery thumbs-down signs.

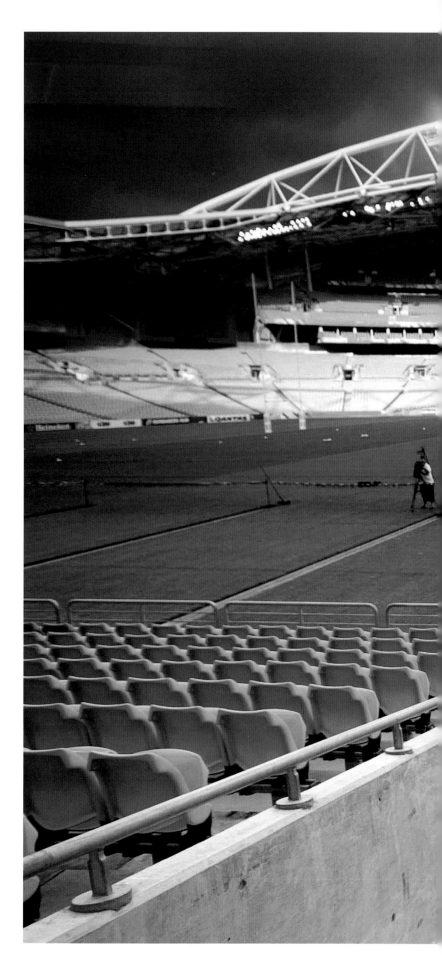

Clive Woodward with assistant Andy
Robinson at England's training session
at Brookvale Oval, Sydney.

Back home, rugby union, a minor deity compared with the great god of football, had captured the public imagination. On that Saturday morning in late November, streets and supermarket aisles stood empty as the nation waited for the breakfast-time kick-off. In front rooms, in rugby clubs, and in pubs, schools and offices opened specially for the occasion, an audience later estimated at 15 million munched their cornflakes and chewed their fingernails. A cinema in the West End of London swapped Hollywood blockbusters for a slice of sporting history from Sydney. Not many of the viewers claimed even a nodding acquaintance with the Laws of the Game, but most of them now knew by sight Johnson, Wilkinson, Dallaglio and the rest. They looked on as Woodward smiled and expressed the hope that everyone would enjoy the occasion, as he intended to do.

Seven of Australia's final squad of 22 knew what it was like to win the Webb Ellis Cup; to "Bring Home Bill", as they expressed it. None of England's starting line-up had done that. Only one – Jason Leonard – had so much as appeared in a final, the defeat by Australia at Twickenham in 1991. Even Johnson, winner of every trophy possible at club level with Leicester, and uniquely twice the captain of the Lions, was breaking new ground. In due course, either he or the nuggety Wallaby scrum-half, George Gregan, would get his hands on the little gold pot at the end of the rainbow.

Fans and pundits weighed up the relative strengths of the finalists. England's starting XV averaged more than 42 caps per man, Australia's 28. The least experienced member of the Wallaby side, Al Baxter, had been called into the front row after a neck injury suffered by Ben Darwin against the All Blacks. In the back three, England looked to Jason Robinson, Josh Lewsey and Ben Cohen to give them wings – they were the Spitfires. Up front Johnson and his heavyweight crew were the Lancaster bombers.

Even though Wilkinson's kicking had occasionally misfired earlier in the tournament, the semi-final had reaffirmed the drop goal as a weapon of mass destruction in the fly-half's arsenal. Strangely, England were the only team to set any store by it. Steve Larkham, the quietly-mannered ACT Brumby at No. 10 for Australia, had managed only one drop goal in 64 Tests, albeit a vitally important one in the 1999 World Cup semi-final at Twickenham. And the Wallabies' first choice place-kicker, Elton Flatley, was no more comfortable with the discipline. Wilkinson, by contrast, had popped over seven drops in his previous five matches, including three against France. There was only one other player in the 2003 World Cup who had scored more than one – and Frenchman Dmitri Yachvili's total was two.

The 128-page $12 (£4) match programme sold out two hours before kick-off. On the cover was a photo of the Webb Ellis Cup with the names of the previous winners – all from the southern hemisphere – clearly visible, engraved on the plinth. England were not just playing for themselves, they were representing half the world! The visiting fans generally rated the Telstra Stadium as better than Twickenham, if only because it took just 30 seconds to order and receive a beer from pumps automated to pour four pints at a time. In the party bars run by the Australian Rugby Union's beer sponsors, a swipe of the credit card was all you needed. The Aussies, who had hosted the Olympic Games here in 2000, knew how to look after their customers.

Not a spare seat was to be had as the teams emerged to the strains of "World in Union", Johnson and Gregan leading the way either side of a small podium bearing the golden trophy, twinkling in the floodlights. The ceremonials were the familiar ones – the two anthems sung operatically and theatrically as they had been throughout the World Cup. England's supporters were mostly seated in the upper tiers. They sang the ubiquitous "Swing Low, Sweet Chariot", and the odd chorus of "You're Only Wearing Yellow 'Cos It's Free" – a reference to the hand-out of Wallaby-coloured jackets to Australian fans during the Lions' tour two years previously. The contenders for the best fancy dress were led by the lads in transportee fatigues, complete with balls and chains.

Battle had hardly been joined in earnest when Australia struck the first blow – a deft kick to the wide left by Larkham taken by Lote Tuqiri above the head of the covering Jason Robinson for a try in the sixth minute. One rugby league recruit over another, Tuqiri's 6ft 3in to Robinson's 5ft 8in made it look easy. Flatley's conversion hit a post, and Australia led 5–0. England drew a breath but no more. David Lyons, one of the Wallaby successes of the tournament at No. 8, gave away a penalty at a ruck and Wilkinson set his sights from around 47 metres. The kick went over, and sighs of relief escaped millions of English mouths. Amazing what a difference a few centimetres either way can make. Then Larkham tackled Cohen without the ball. England had got away with a couple of those in previous matches, but Larkham did not, and Wilkinson made it 6–5. It was a lead they would never lose, but a chance to extend it was lost when Wilkinson put a left-footed drop goal attempt wide in the 23rd minute.

Soon after, an even bigger calamity for the challengers: Wilkinson's tackle forced the ball from Matt Giteau's grasp – the replacement fly-half was on for Larkham, who had to make three trips to the blood bin for running repairs to a cut on the chin – and it reached Dawson. The scrum-half was a mere two metres from the line, and had Ben Kay at his right shoulder. It was the equivalent of an open goal in football, or a run-out in cricket with both batsmen stuck in the middle of the pitch. Dawson made the pass but Kay fumbled the ball to the floor. Television replays appeared to show a fractional hesitation on Dawson's part. Was he betrayed subconsciously by a back's instinctive lack of faith in a big forward? Perhaps it was a trick of the eye. Whatever the case, England soon made it 9–5 with a penalty from Wilkinson from a narrow angle, but Kay took a while to regain his composure.

England had other problems, too. They were confident of an ascendancy in the scrum, yet towards the end of the first quarter they had been penalised by South African referee Andre Watson, whose touch judge, the New Zealander Paul Honiss, was finding fault with Woodman's binding. One of the most important ways of getting the whip hand over your opponents is to force them into retreat at the scrum. It became more and more a source of annoyance to England that Watson was seeing things a different way. It was a struggle for them to stay calm. But stay calm they did, and a try of stunning simplicity and cool execution was the reward. The favourite short side approach worked a treat as Dallaglio thundered forward on the left, supported by Wilkinson who snapped a pass outside for Robinson to score at the corner. It was Wendell Sailor's territory to defend, but the ex-rugby league man had been caught out of position. "We scored against Sailor, in his corner, three games in a row," observed Andy Robinson later. "Twickenham in November 2002, Melbourne in June and then the final. We knew there was a weakness there and we were able to exploit it. It was a great try." Jason Robinson, exultant, punched the air and screamed "Come on!" Up in the stands, England's royal fan, Prince Harry, hugged Clive Woodward's wife, Jayne.

It was a minor consideration at the time but Wilkinson might, in fact, have given the scoring pass inside to Cohen, which would have made the conversion easier. The kick went wide, so England led 14–5 at half-time, and they would have happily played on for a few more minutes, with Australia struggling. The consensus in the England changing room was that simple, tight rugby would win them the cup. Keep the error count down, and the points would come.

But Australia had not defeated the All Blacks through meek submission and they came out fighting for the second half. An over-throw by Steve Thompson at a line-out led to a scramble and a Wallaby penalty; Flatley made it 14–8. A few minutes later the same man was a fraction short of another three points after Dawson and Josh Lewsey were whistled up for crossing. This was Australia's time. With an hour played, Vickery scrabbled for the ball on the ground and Flatley converted his second penalty to cut England's advantage to 14–11. Wilkinson dragged Larkham down by his shorts to stop a breakthrough. At the other end, Mat Rogers slid in to scoop the ball away from Will Greenwood and stifle a rare English raid. After 72 minutes, Wilkinson dropped for goal again – and missed again. Cue more gasps in the stands.

Referee Watson had twice awarded penalties against England's scrum during the second half. The South African was driving Johnson to distraction. "You've got to ping the three!" shouted the captain, who felt that Baxter (No. 3 for Australia) was getting away with dropping the scrum. Instead Watson, in the final minute, made a hugely dramatic intervention. At a scrum in England's half, Woodman stayed standing instead of combining with Thompson and Vickery to engage with the opposing front row. Woodman argued that the Australians went in early. Ordinarily, the two packs would have been asked to re-engage. Watson whistled for a penalty against England.

The kick would have been tricky enough in a training session. That Flatley put it over with such wonderful composure was worthy of winning any match, let alone sending one into extra time.

England's supporters were stunned but had to applaud the nerve of the man. "People say you can shut out the noise of the crowd, but it's rubbish," said Wilkinson. "You can hear the crowd all the time, you just have to understand that it doesn't matter – if you don't want it to." Woodward left his coach's booth to join the players on the field. He went to Wilkinson and spoke to him for a few seconds, but got an unexpected response. "Yeah, yeah, I've got it," the fly-half said. "But I've got to go and practise my kicking." Amid the tension, the coach could not help but smile.

In 1966, Alf Ramsey told his team before extra time against West Germany: "You've won it once, now go and do it again." Johnson's

message, according to Dawson, was: "Fellas, you have worked your whole career for the next 20 minutes. Don't waste it." The captain gestured over to the Wallabies, who were looking tired and drained. Woodward said: "Stop coughing up the ball and keep defending as you are." England took Vickery off and sent on Jason Leonard. If the scores were still level after extra time there would be a further 10 minutes of sudden death. Looming after that was a drop goal shoot-out, with five different kickers from each team.

Two minutes in, Wilkinson lined up a daunting kick from 45 metres out towards the right-hand touchline. Defying the wind and the rain, he made it 17–14, and allowed himself a small puff of the cheeks as he ran back. Amazingly, for all Johnson's magnificent efforts, it was England's first score since the Jason Robinson try in the first half. Play went on. The two sides were living on their instincts and their nerves. If ever Dave "Otis" Reddin's fitness regime would count for something, it was now. In the second period of extra time, with bodies scattered everywhere and two minutes left until sudden death, Dallaglio was judged to have used his hands illegally in a ruck. Extraordinarily to those who did not know rugby, the square-jawed Wasp's reaction was not to rant and rave against the decision, but to turn quietly away from the referee and shake his head. Flatley converted the kick. Once more it was all square, at 17–17. Could neither side close the deal?

Zig Zag

England had a call for it, of course, like they had a call for every planned move. The call was "Zig zag". It might never have happened if Mat Rogers, the Wallaby full-back, had shown the same calmness as Flatley. Instead Rogers, collecting Wilkinson's long drop-out in Australia's 22, failed to get good distance on a clearing kick to touch, and gave England a line-out within decent range of the posts. Those with the coolest of minds might have recalled at that moment a similar situation involving the same countries at the 1995 World Cup, when Rob Andrew dropped a goal to win a quarter-final in Cape Town. Now, Andrew was seated alongside Ian Robertson, the former Scotland international commentating on the final for BBC Radio. Both men knew what was coming. "Wilkinson will drop for goal," said Robertson. Lewis Moody, on as a substitute for Hill, took the line-out throw from Thompson. England moved into midfield and were held up in the tackle. Dawson shaped as if to pass then, in a moment of intuitive brilliance, darted through a gap to move a precious 20 metres nearer the target. Dawson was tackled and tied up. Seeing this, Neil Back and Martin Johnson did what came naturally, and with short drives forward bought a few more metres. On the bench, Andy Gomarsall grabbed Woodward's arm: "We're going to do it, we're going to do it." Dawson recovered his position, and his poise. He fired possibly the sweetest pass of his career, and certainly of the final, to the waiting Wilkinson in the "pocket" behind him. Robertson's words tracked the trajectory of the ball: "There's offside, surely; no, Martin Johnson has it. He drives, there's 35 seconds to go. This is the one, it's coming back for Jonny Wilkinson. He drops for World Cup glory. It's up. It's over! [Cue a banshee screech from Andrew]. He's done it! Jonny

Will Greenwood leaves an impromptu photocall outside the team hotel in Manly ahead of the World Cup final against Australia.

Jonny Wilkinson in his Manly hotel room takes a break from his favourite form of relaxation, playing guitar.

Wilkinson is England's hero, yet again. And there's no time for Australia to come back."

It was an instantly memorable piece of commentary, as Wilkinson's right boot smoothly and sweetly dispatched the ball between the posts, banishing thoughts of his earlier misses and vindicating all those countless hours of practice. "Who else would you want to see behind you," said Johnson later, "waiting to drop a goal to win a trophy?" Wilkinson swapped a high five with Iain Balshaw, who was on for Lewsey.

But there was, despite Robertson's words, time for an Australian riposte. And again, the Wallabies fell short of what was required. Their chasers needed a fighting chance to retrieve the ball from the kick-off, but it was fielded instead by Woodman, of all people, in space. England rucked it back, and ferried it to Mike Catt, another substitute. "Kick it to the shithouse," bellowed Dawson, and Catt did as he was instructed. The final kick of the final match soared into the crowd to herald the final whistle. Wilkinson leapt in the air, yelling "World Cup, World Cup!" The fans, to a man and woman, hugged each other. The anxiety had been immense and its release brought a flood of emotion; many burst into tears. The scene was the same in the tented villages set up in Sydney for those without tickets, and back home in the pubs, clubs and front rooms. A notable exception to the rule was Mrs Philippa Wilkinson, Jonny's mum, who was too nervous to watch and was eventually trailed by reporters to her local supermarket in Northumberland, where workers on the vegetable counter delivered the good news.

Johnson spoke with dignity to a television interviewer. "I'm happy for our players because they put so much into it. We have got to give credit to Australia. It couldn't have been any closer and I'm just happy to be on the right side." Gregan acknowledged Wilkinson's efforts: "He knocked over the one that counted and you've got to take your hat off to him. It was a massive final, wasn't it? Congratulations to England. They delivered under pressure and they delivered when it counted."

It took an age for the Australian Prime Minister, John Howard, and the IRB chairman, Syd Millar, to hand out the medals, with the entire squads including the support staff of the winners and losers filing past on a raised dais on the pitch. Millar was virtually throwing the medals at them by the end. At last Johnson took delivery of the cup that was the cause of all the fuss. With a smile lighting up his stubbly, bloody, battered features, he turned, hoisted it to the heavens and shouted one word: "Yes!"

The players set off round the pitch to parade their spoils, and family and friends came down to join in. The supporters sang "Swing Low" again and "Wonderwall", the favourite of the 1997 Lions. Woodward embraced his wife and children. "That moment," he said, "when Johnson lifted the cup, was when you went 'Wow, we've done it'." In the changing rooms, it was a private kind of bedlam. Prince Harry embraced Johnson, who asked him "Did you enjoy it?" The prince's beaming smile suggested that he had. John Howard offered his congratulations. "Great game, epic game," said the PM, with a great grimace, epic grimace. For the next two hours around the ground it was impossible to get a signal on a mobile telephone.

On any other occasion, Woodward and Andy Robinson would have pored over the video tape of the match within hours, dissecting and digesting. They did have a brief word with Watson about his refereeing of the scrum, but this was no time for taking things too seriously. There were official niceties to attend to in the next two days, but for once the letting-down of hair took precedence. An organised function at the Opium Bar overlooking the Opera House moved on to the Cargo Bar where Prince Harry was sighted again, and the Hyatt Hotel. Steve Thompson proposed to his girlfriend, Fiona, on Manly Beach and was accepted. "It was like winning the World Cup all over again," Thompson said. Leonard, Paul Grayson and Martin Corry amused the crowd gathered outside the team hotel on the Sunday afternoon by cadging a lift back in a police van after a particularly monstrous session. That evening, Wilkinson was named Player of the Year at the International Rugby Board awards dinner, in succession to Fabien Galthié. Afterwards the players repaired to Darling Harbour for rather more informal festivities.

On the Monday, the squad gathered on the beach to be photographed in their club jerseys for a cannily imaginative photograph to be used in publicity material for the domestic game. (If you ever see the photo, check out Dan Luger lurking at the back, in a sweatshirt. Having already signed for Perpignan in France, he was the odd man out). At his final debrief, Woodward addressed the squad; his world champion squad. The air of satisfaction mingled with the expected after-effects of a night on the tiles. "One thing to remember," said the coach. "Around here, they call it Bill. We don't. It's the World Cup and that's is how we'll always describe it." It was the last instruction of a long, long list. And have you ever yet heard an England player call it anything else?

In years to come, just as football fans could reel off the names of the '66 winners – Banks, Cohen, Wilson, Jackie Charlton, Moore and so on – so rugby's followers would do the same. Woodman, Thompson, Vickery; Johnson and Kay; Hill, Back, Dallaglio; Dawson and Wilkinson; Greenwood, Tindall, Cohen, Robinson, Lewsey. The substitutes used in the final were Leonard, Moody, Catt and Balshaw.

The Boy's Own outcome to it all elevated Wilkinson immediately from local hero to cast-iron national celebrity. Johnson was England's first World Cup-winning captain since Moore in 1966, and Woodward was tipped for a knighthood as the whole squad was teed up to receive the thanks of a success-starved nation. First, though, they had to get home.

An Australian fan watches the first semi-final of the Rugby World Cup against New Zealand.

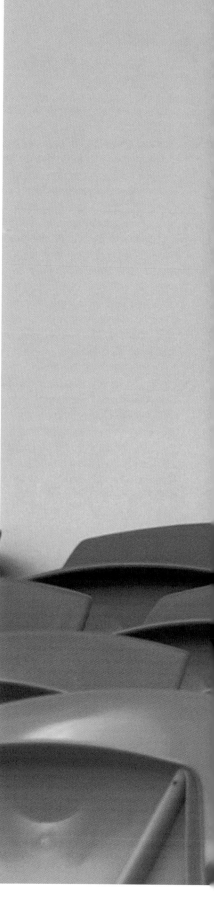

Above Jason Leonard interviewed in the Hilton Hotel after being named in the starting line-up for the quarter final against Wales, thus equalling the world record for international caps in rugby.

Right The great communicator – Clive Woodward talks on the phone during a training session at the Suncorp Stadium in Brisbane.

Left Martin Johnson practises his ball skills.

Above Jonny Wilkinson and Simon Shaw in training in Brisbane.

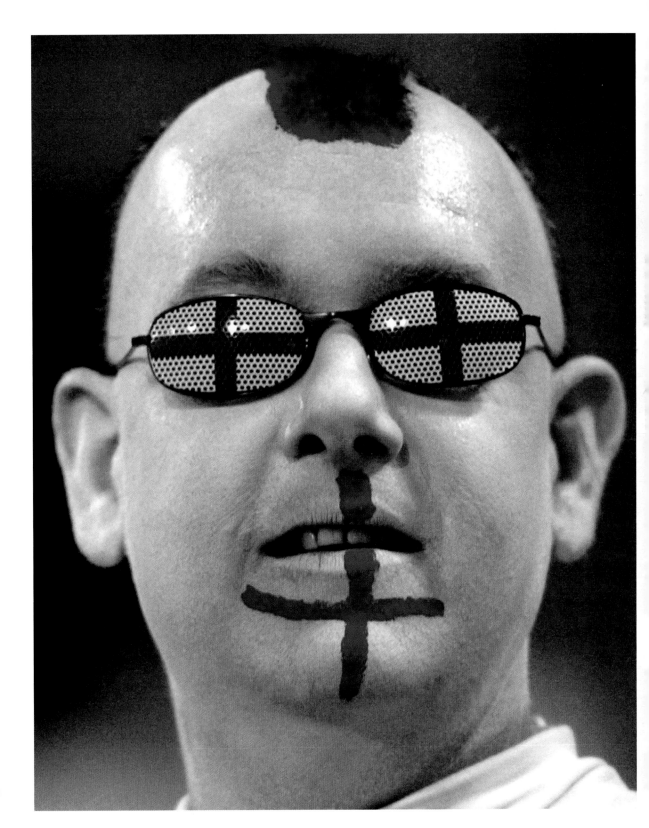

Left England fans watch the quarter-final against Wales in Brisbane.

Right An England fan wearing face paint and England glasses at the quarter-final.

Overleaf Clive Woodward looks on anxiously as Wales lead England during the first half.

An England fan celebrates during the
England v Wales quarter-final match
in Brisbane.

Martin Johnson takes a breather during
a penalty goal attempt against Wales.

Left Lewis Moody grabs the ball in a line-out against Wales' Martyn Williams.

Above Dan Luger is tackled by scrum-half Gareth Cooper.

Mark Jones of Wales fails to shrug off
Phil Vickery.

Welsh wing Shane Williams gives a
flying Jonny Wilkinson the brush-off.

Above Jonny Wilkinson and Stephen Jones in an aerial battle of fly-halfs.

Right Jason Robinson gets past Stephen Jones and Jonathan Thomas to set up England's try against Wales.

Above Will Greenwood scores the England try against Wales.

Right Jonny Wilkinson lands a drop goal as Wales are finally quashed at Brisbane.

Downtime before the sem-final – Ben
Kay samples the life of the surfer on
Manly Beach.

Above Trevor Woodman, Jason Leonard and Mark Regan in training at the Telstra Stadium in Sydney.

Right Ben Cohen and Lawrence Dallaglio on the run at the same training session.

Mike Tindall in a quiet moment during
training at Sydney's Brookvale Oval.

Neil Back faces the press in Sydney
before the semi-final against France.

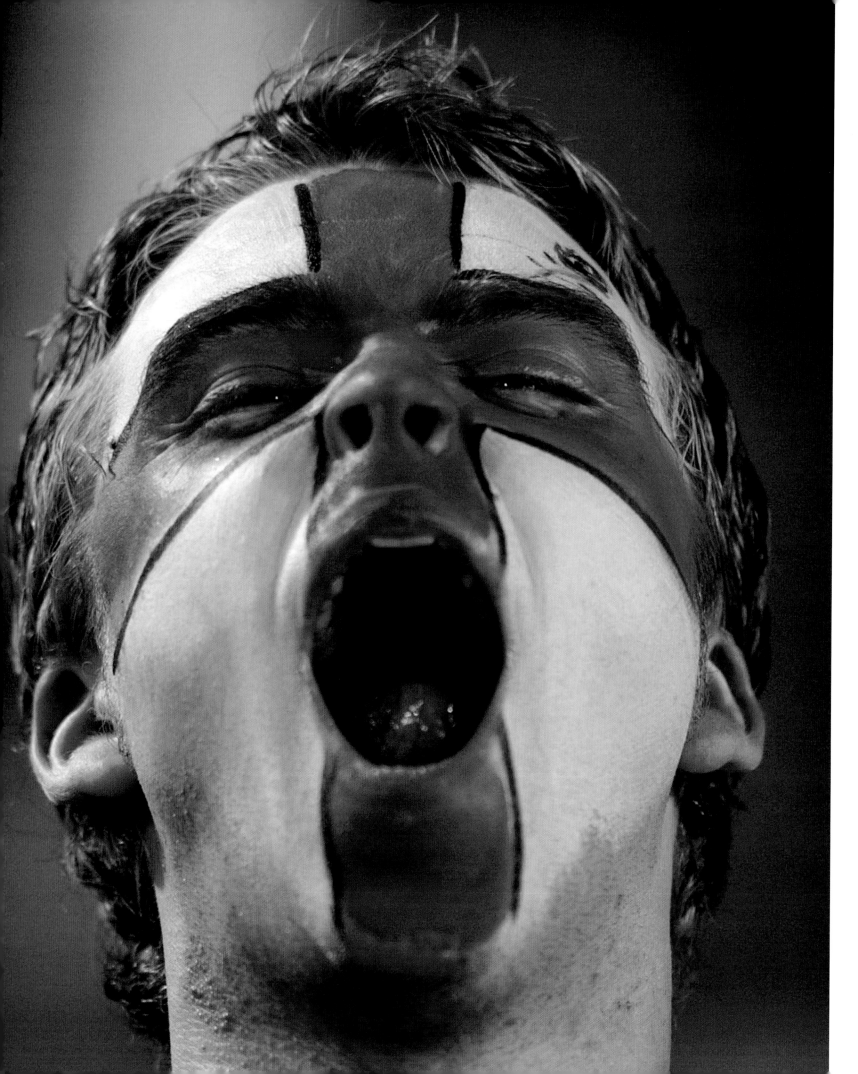

Left An England fan gets in the spirit before the match with France.

Above French fans before the semi-final against England.

Left England sing their national anthem before the France game.

Above Martin Johnson delivers final instructions on the game plan to beat the French.

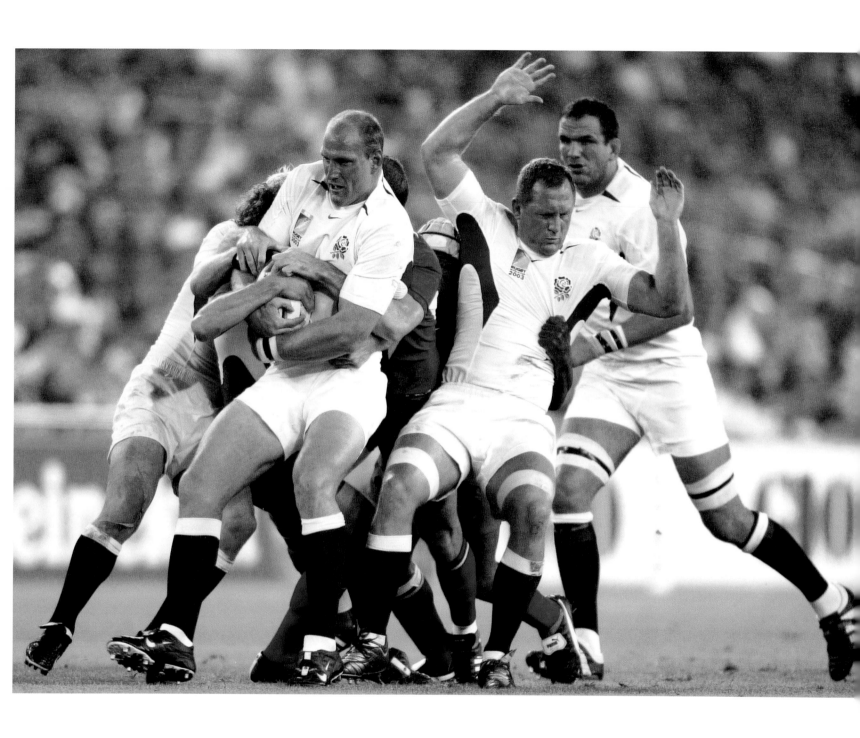

Above Lawrence Dallaglio and the returning Richard Hill in the thick of the semi-final action.

Right A French fan looks on during the semi-final against England.

A "ludicrous challenge" – Christophe Dominici's trip injured the France wing himself while sending Jason Robinson flying. Dominici was sent to the sin bin and did not return.

Lawrence Dallaglio hangs on to Imanol Harinordoquy, dubbed by some "Harry Ordinary" for his semi-final showing.

Above Ben Cohen looks for support as he is tackled by Imanol Harinordoquy.

Right Neil Back makes a break against France.

Left Jonny Wilkinson is grounded after a late tackle by Serge Betsen.

Right Serge Betsen leaves the field after being shown a yellow card.

The semi-final is going England's way at the Telstra Stadium. The final score is 24–7 to England.

Left Josh Lewsey has a swim at Manly Beach in Sydney the day after the semi-final victory against France.

Above England fans reserve a large space on the sand.

Richard Hill, Trevor Woodman and Ben Kay take part in an icy recovery session at Harbord Diggers Pool in Manly.

Above England did not hide away before the final – Martin Johnson in demand for photos and autographs after a swim at Manly Beach.

Right Neil Back signs autographs on Manly Beach.

Left Dorian West and Martin Johnson training at Brookvale Oval, Sydney.

Above "England went into the final almost taken aback at their relaxed state of mind" – Martin Johnson attends a news conference at the team's hotel in Manly before the World Cup final.

Left Clive Woodward walks past policemen providing security after a training session at Brookvale Oval.

Right Clive Woodward in pensive mood at a press conference.

Lawrence Dallaglio is happy to take a photo for a Japanese tourist in front of the Sydney Harbour Bridge.

Left Final preparations – Jonny Wilkinson deep in concentration as he walks out to practise kicking at the Telstra Stadium the day before the Rugby World Cup final.

Above Jonny Wilkinson with kicking coach Dave Alred.

The Telstra Stadium hosts the Rugby
World Cup final.

Left The two captains, Martin Johnson and George Gregan, lead out their teams.

Right An England fan with a message for her Australian counterparts.

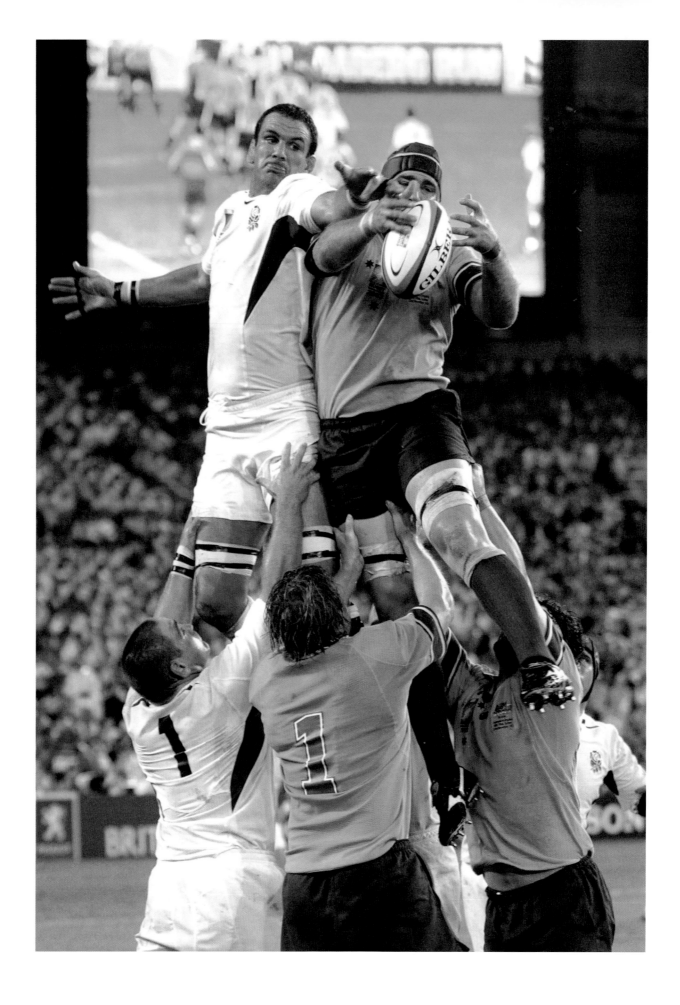

Left Martin Johnson and David Lyons contest a line-out during the final.

Right Jonny Wilkinson tackles Matt Giteau of Australia, who was used three times as a blood replacement for Steve Larkham.

Above The first blow is struck – Lote Tuqiri of Australia takes a high ball over Jason Robinson to score the opening try of the final.

Right Stirling Mortlock, Lote Tuqiri and Elton Flatley of Australia celebrate.

Martin Johnson rallies his team after
they fall behind to Tuqiri's touchdown.

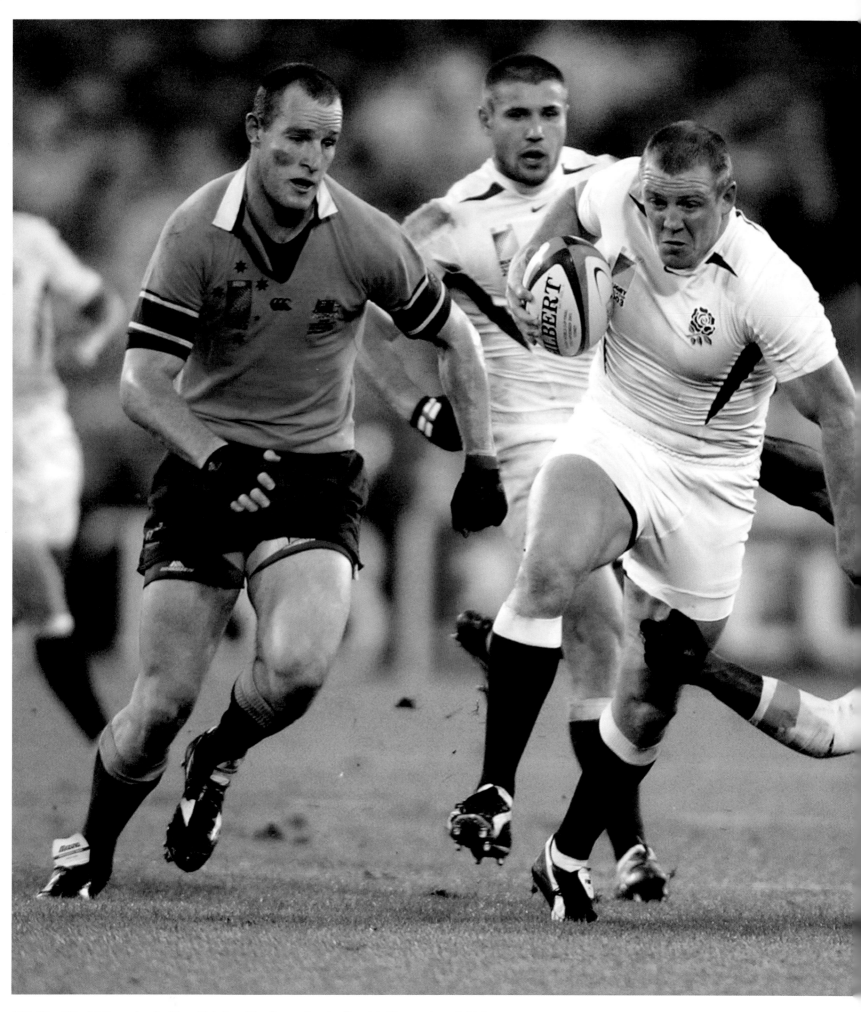

Mike Tindall breaks the tackle of
Wendell Sailor with Jason Robinson
in support.

Left An English fan yells for his team.

Right Ben Cohen is wrapped up by the Australian defence.

"A try of stunning simplicity and cool execution" – Jonny Wilkinson passes outside to Jason Robinson (left), and the England wing is over the line before Mat Rogers and Wendell Sailor can stop him (right and overleaf).

Above Matt Dawson gets the ball away from a scrum, a highly controversial area in the final.

Right Martin Johnson and Ben Kay hold Australia back as the ball comes out to Matt Dawson.

Above Lote Tuqiri of Australia and
Josh Lewsey contest a loose ball.

Right Clive Woodward issues
instructions to Jonny Wilkinson before
the start of extra time.

Wallaby flanker Phil Waugh tries to find a
hole in the defence.

Australia's head coach Eddie Jones
looks on during the final.

Concern on the face of an England fan
as extra time continues.

With seconds left on the clock, Jonny Wilkinson prepares to drop kick into rugby history.

Jonny Wilkinson's kick sails over between the posts as Phil Waugh attempts a chargedown.

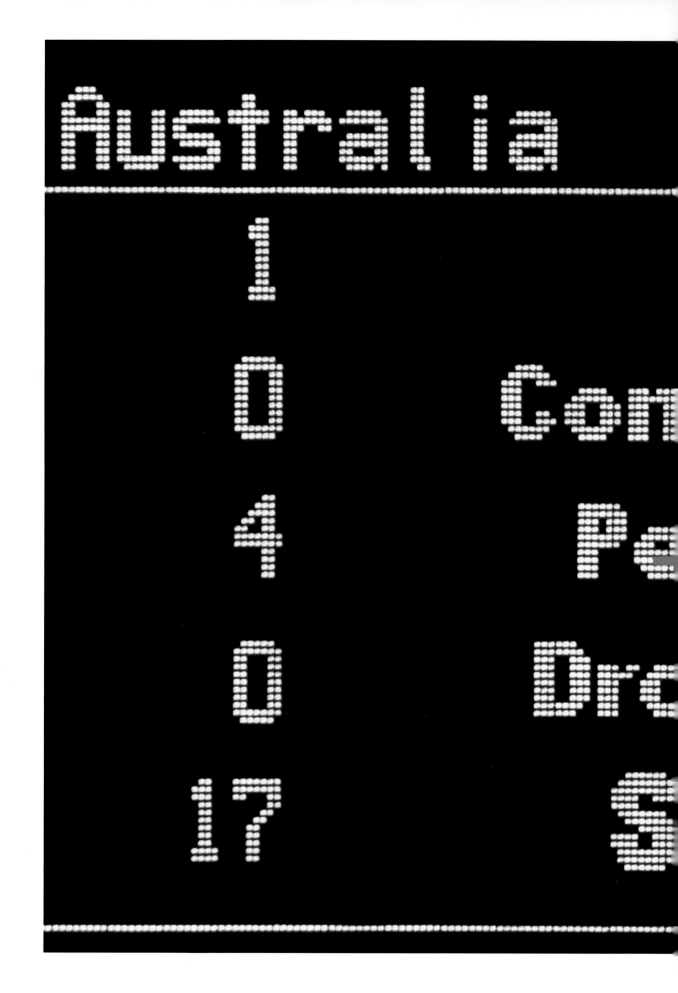

The scoreboard tells the story.

The final whistle – Martin Johnson,
Neil Back and Trevor Woodman
celebrate, while Jonny Wilkinson is
ecstatic (right).

Above England players celebrate
surrounded by dejected Wallabies.

Right Will Greenwood drops to his
knees, a world champion.

Winners and losers – Australian
fans drown their sorrows (left) after
Wilkinson's winning kick while
England supporters in fancy dress
celebrate (above).

Josh Lewsey, Kyran Bracken, Mike Catt, Jonny Wilkinson, Richard Hill, Matt Dawson and Ben Kay line up to receive the winners' medals.

Above Deposed world champion
Wallabies Brendan Cannon, Bill Young,
Elton Flatley and Wendell Sailor after
the match.

Right Mike Catt and Jonny Wilkinson
in raptures as Martin Johnson shows
them the ultimate rugby prize.

Left England captain Martin Johnson holds aloft the Webb Ellis Cup.

Right The Catt that got the cream.

Matt Dawson celebrates with Ben Cohen (left), while the front row union – Phil Vickery, Steve Thompson and Trevor Woodman – savour the moment (right).

Dallaglio on the victory lap of honour.

Above The wives and girlfriends of the
England players join in the celebrations
on the pitch.

Right Martin Johnson kisses his wife in
front of photographers.

Jonny Wilkinson is congratulated by England fans as he goes down the players' tunnel after the win over Australia.

Left "This is what we came for" – Clive Woodward shows off the World Cup.

Above An unusual celebration by an England fan after the final.

Clive Woodward with the Webb Ellis
Cup after the match.

Victory Celebrations

Victory Celebrations

The mere mortals in the Sydney departure hall a little under two days after Martin Johnson collected the World Cup soon spotted the huge trunks bearing the names of the men whose every move they had followed for the previous six weeks. As the plane carrying the England team home soared into the Monday evening sky the captain announced its renaming as "Sweet Chariot" and advised the passengers: "When the seat-belt sign is switched off, the World Cup will be coming your way." Jason Leonard and Matt Dawson brought the cup down one aisle of the Jumbo, then Lawrence Dallaglio and Ben Cohen looked after the other. The passengers took photos of the players with the trophy. Then the players took photos of the passengers with the trophy. "Don't worry," said the captain, "it's a long way to Singapore."

It is doubtful whether the England squad thought this would be the limit to the back-slapping and hand-shaking, but none of them was prepared for what was to follow. The truth dawned, before dawn, the next day on arrival at Heathrow. "We were told they'd take us into arrivals four or five at a time," said Matt Dawson. "We thought: 'What are you on about?'" What the police at Terminal Four were on about was hundreds of well-wishers flocking to welcome the team home. Neil Back marched into the arrivals area, Webb Ellis Cup held high in one hand. What a lapse in planning: they should have given it to Simon Shaw, who at 6ft 9in would have given the crowd a better view. A little later at Pennyhill Park, where the squad enjoyed a restorative and very English fry-up, weary eyes blinked at the media's flashbulbs and arc lights. Questions, questions, mostly variations on the theme of "How do you feel?" Well, pretty good, as it happens, but we couldn't half do with some sleep.

The idea was soon hatched of a victory parade on an open-topped bus through London, and the date was set for Monday 8 December. The Queen and the Prime Minister, Tony Blair, invited the team to receptions later the same day. It allowed less than a fortnight to work out a route and take care of security. When it came, the players were uncertain what scale the celebrations would take. "No one's going to turn up in this, it's freezing out there," said Jason Leonard as he met up with Lawrence Dallaglio and Mike Catt for breakfast, before joining the squad at Twickenham to be taken to the start of the parade at the Intercontinental Hotel in Park Lane. There were three buses: one for the players, one for the coaches and support staff, and one for the media. "We were just having a laugh," said Leonard, "Gentle banter about what was to come. The shock came when we first got round to Marble Arch." Passing under the Arch and turning right into Oxford Street, the convoy was greeted by a throng of humanity stretching as far as the eye could see. The buses slowed to the pace of a rolling maul as the stunned players cheered and waved for all they were worth.

It was a staggering turnout. From all over the country they had come to join London's men in suits on lunch breaks, and office, shop and restaurant workers grabbing a sly half hour. People hung out of windows, clambered onto bus shelters, swung from traffic lights and lampposts. Along Oxford Street, into Regent Street, across Piccadilly Circus and down Haymarket to Trafalgar Square: the crowd was estimated at three quarters of a million. At

Previous pages Thousands of rugby fans gather in London's Trafalgar Square to welcome the England team on their victory parade.

Above England captain Martin Johnson with the Webb Ellis Cup.

the end of the 45-minute journey, Nelson's Column rose out of the crowd like Excalibur from a lake of red-and-white. Those at the front where Clive Woodward and the players made speeches of thanks had been queuing all night. A topical point of conversation at the time was what to do with the empty plinth alongside Landseer's lions. The consensus was obvious – a bronze of Martin Johnson would do nicely.

Returning to the Intercontinental Hotel, Woodward was at his most relaxed and carefree. He began with a self-deprecatory quip about his choice of the team's garb – the grey suits which had made their debut at the send-off dinner in September – on a freezing morning. "No coats on the bus, bad call!" Woodward said. "You know, the scenes at the hotel in Manly, the scenes in the stadium in Sydney, the scenes at Heathrow: they've all been fantastic. But this was just something I don't think any of us were really expecting at all. It was just incredible, amazing. Trafalgar Square summed up the whole thing, but from the moment we started it was incredible. And it's been all over the country, I think. I've had thousands and thousands of letters. I'd just give a massive thank you to everyone who got behind the team; it's brilliant."

The future, though, is only ever a heartbeat away. Mike Tindall had put it succinctly, saying: "Four years' work, what the f*** are we going to do now?" Already, the talk was of Johnson and a couple of the other more senior citizens calling it quits. Chris Hewett of *The Independent* asked Woodward whether there was one small voice saying "We've achieved this – what now?" The reply was immediate. "No, not at all. For one or two players it might be that, but my role and the staff's role is to give this group of players every chance of being successful. We gave them every possible chance to be in a situation where there are no excuses, that they could do it on any given day, and they've taken that. I think for me, and I speak for Andy Robinson and Phil Larder, it was hugely satisfying but that's what we do as a job and as a career. We have to move on."

The Queen greeted the squad at Buckingham Palace and while an official photograph was taken, the royal corgis were allowed to sniff the brown shoes which more or less went with the grey suits. Then it was on to Downing Street, with Leonard jauntily holding the cup in one hand as he led the way to the PM's place. Lawrence Dallaglio deviated from his coach's line slightly, saying: "People are so quick to take away the result and say you've got to think about the next game. But you've got to treasure those memories. They'll live with you for the rest of your life, and you must cherish them dearly."

In addition to the ceremonial splendour, there was hard commercial business to take care of. A flurry of books hurried onto the stalls, including *Sweet Chariot*, the official book of the tournament, laced with advertisements. Within days of the final, 160,000 copies of *Martin Johnson: The Autobiography* went on sale, featuring the captain and the trophy on the cover, and a rapidly-penned closing chapter describing the final. Sales eventually ran to around a quarter of a million: a huge total for any sports book, never mind one about a rugby player. There were four official video compilations, although the full rerun of the final did not appear until well into 2004. Phil Vickery put the finishing touches to his video diary of the year, *Champion! From Tears to*

Former Wallaby David Campese lost a bet and did a "walk of shame" down Oxford Street in London.

Triumph, and Matt Dawson also went into print with his autobiography, *Nine Lives*. Dawson, in common with Dallaglio, had a round of benefit dinners to attend to, and the scrum-half's best story was soon dozens of times into the telling. When passing through security at Sydney Airport, Dawson kept setting off the metal detector buzzer. He fished his keys and coins out of his pockets, and still the buzzer went. Finally he reached under his shirt and pulled out his World Cup medal. Panic over, cobber.

The influence of the World Cup spread far and wide. Interestingly, rugby union was held up as a model for other sports, with high earners in football often suffering unfavourable comparisons. Michael Parkinson, writing in *The Daily Telegraph*, gave a typical view: "In all the talk about lessons to be learned surely the most important of all was that a game, one which is played, regulated and watched in a civilised manner, can lift our hearts and remind us of how things ought to be. It demonstrated how multitudes of people can make fun as well as unforgettable drama out of fierce rivalries providing they bear in mind the essential truth that when all is said and done what they are partaking in is an entertainment."

The rest of sporting life in England took a back seat, as everyone got involved in rugby, from bards and artists to anyone hoping to make a fast buck. The Poet Laureate, Andrew Motion, was moved to pen a four-verse tribute in the limerick style. It began: "O Jonny the power of your boot/ And the accurate heart-stopping route/ Of your goal as it ghosts/ Through Australian posts/ Is a triumph we gladly salute." Darren Baker, a 27-year-old artist from Yorkshire, captured the Wilkinson drop goal in pastels and oils. Baker, it was reported, applied "the techniques of the 17th-century Old Masters to resolutely contemporary subjects". His Wilkinson work went on display at the Halcyon Gallery in London's Mayfair, and the artist described the difference between his work and that of a photographer: "It's the chiaroscuro. Light and dark. It gives a presence to paintings, and a depth."

There was an extraordinary depth to people's pockets, too. A memorabilia market sprang up immediately, with a square foot of earth from the Telstra Stadium pitch put up for sale on eBay, and earning a four-figure sum for London's Great Ormond Street Children's Hospital. More spectacular was the £500,000 paid by Philip Green, owner of Bhs and Arcadia, for a signed shirt worn by Dorian West, England's replacement hooker in the final who did not even get on to the field. Dawson's jersey from the final was auctioned for £12,000 at a 720-seat dinner at London's Royal Lancaster Hotel. With ordinary autographed jerseys routinely fetching £500, players had to become more aware of what they were signing, and for whom.

According to PR adviser Max Clifford, they had to start watching what they said, too. Jonny Wilkinson was asked whether his success meant he would be recognised now in a branch of McDonald's. The fly-half replied that he hadn't been in one for years. Bad move, said Clifford. An honest answer, said many others. McDonald's had a better idea anyway: they paid Dallaglio to appear in a television advertisement, demanding "110 per cent" from his burger, whatever that meant. But it was light-hearted, and an indication that rugby's leading lights might cross into the mainstream hitherto occupied by football's Beckhams and Owens. The nation's kids ensured that *World*

Championship Rugby, Official Game of the England Rugby Team leapt into the best-seller list for PlayStation 2, PC and XBox formats.

Plans had been put in place before the end of the World Cup for a celebration game at Twickenham, though fearing the inevitable accusation of arrogance, the RFU kept it quiet. With the trophy safely secured, a non-cap match against the New Zealand Barbarians five days before Christmas was announced. The 75,000 tickets went in a flash, even though England's squad was an off-the-cuff, ad hoc collection of five of the World Cup final team, eight more squad members from Australia and a number of international wannabes including James Simpson-Daniel, Ollie Smith, Andy Titterrell and Matt Stevens. Without being unkind to Ben Gollings, the sevens specialist who made it onto the England bench, it was Johnson, Wilkinson and Dallaglio that the crowd wanted to see. They got their way, but only at the end of an oddly-shaped match in chilly conditions. As on the day of the victory parade, the feelgood factor merged with the feel-cold factor.

There was a curious mix of attacking verve from both sides and some calculated violence from the Barbarians' Troy Flavell. The All Black lock was cited and banned for four weeks for various misdemeanours including breaking the nose of Richard Hill – a fine souvenir for the proud captain for the evening. England's pick-up XV won 42–17, and then the World Cup squad from Sydney emerged onto the floodlit Twickenham pitch for a lap of honour. Martin Johnson flew in by helicopter from Northampton, where he had played in a club match for Leicester earlier in the day; the captain wore a winter overcoat, others were in tracksuits, and poor Lewis Moody hobbled around on crutches, with a stress fracture of the foot. It looked more like the retreat from Moscow than a triumphal return from down under. But the crowd lapped it up all the same, as the standards "Swing Low" and "The Great Escape" blared out over the loudspeakers.

The Newspaper Publishers' Association published an advertisement claiming that "twice as many men read about the World Cup than watched it on television". But the goggle-box was a useful medium for the new England fans to gain familiarity with their heroes. Comedian Harry Hill spoke on behalf of the converts, who wouldn't have known a Wasp from a Harlequin a couple of months previously, in his *TV Burp* programme a few days after the final. "I didn't watch it really," he confided in an aside to camera, "I'm just pretending I did to keep in with people. But I was delighted when Jonny kicked the ball, er, up…"

Over at the BBC – otherwise known as the World Cup-free channel – the *Sports Review of the Year* was a takeover for England. They won the Team of the Year award and the Personality of the Year was Wilkinson (although many rugby die-hards would have given it to Johnson). Before the summer tour, Wilkinson had been available at odds of 8–1 to win the award. Nice work for those who got it. But the Beeb struck a duff note by inviting the world's most notorious Pom-basher, the former Wallaby wing David Campese, to present the team award. Campese, casually dressed, rubbed shoulders uncomfortably with the England team, still wearing those grey suits. Dawson's jacket was showing severe signs of wear, with the hem below the pocket sagging like a dog's tongue on a hot day. A couple of days later, a seething Woodward labelled the choice of Campese as

Paul Grayson, Jonny Wilkinson and Mark Regan share a joke during a photo shoot in their club jerseys on Manly Beach.

"crass" and condemned the corporation for ignoring more suitable candidates, including Sir Bobby Charlton and the Princess Royal, both of whom were in attendance. "It's typical of British sport that the moment you achieve something fantastic, someone tries to make a joke of it," Woodward said. Josh Lewsey, contributing his weekly column to the *Metro* newspaper, took a different tack, saying it was "amazingly satisfying" to have Campese "of all people" to present the award. The feisty Australian, for his part, ate a long overdue slice of humble pie – albeit at the behest of his bookmaker sponsor – by walking down Oxford Street carrying a sandwich board that read: "I admit, the best team won!"

Keeping the oval ball rolling, and altogether more gushing in its praise, was an offering on ITV, recorded the day after the BBC's *Sports Review* and shown the following Saturday evening. *We are the Champions: The Nation Celebrates* was hosted by Chris Tarrant, and attended by the entire squad and the kind of celebrity audience that more usually pitches up for Dame Edna Everage or Billy Connolly. It is certainly a rare event that sets Steve Thompson alongside Antony Worrall Thompson. The grand finale had Heather Small singing "Search for the Hero Inside Yourself" – purportedly the squad's favourite tune of inspiration, though there were a few befuddled looks from the players perched awkwardly on the stage nearby in, of course, those grey suits.

If the private whispers among the squad described the programme as "tacky", Jonny Wilkinson was far happier, by all accounts, with the more dignified civic reception in Newcastle, when he received the Freedom of the City – an honorary Geordiehood, no less. It was a popular gesture all over the country, and there had not been so many newly free men walking around since the abolition of slavery. Phil Vickery, Trevor Woodman and Andy Gomarsall accepted the freedom of Gloucester, and the two props were feted in Truro, county town of their native Cornwall. The Northampton contingent of Dawson, Cohen, Thompson and Grayson were similarly honoured, and in Rugby, the cradle of the game, the entire England squad were given the freedom of the town. Clive Woodward headed up a delegation at the Town Hall, and told the gathering: "We are delighted to accept this honour on behalf of all the squad. I am fully aware this does not give us the right to drive sheep up the high street but if any parking fines could be waived that would be great!" The motion by Council Leader Craig Humphrey, in the Temple Speech Rooms, was passed without dissent, and actor Nick Bailey (aka Dr Trueman in *EastEnders*) read out Andrew Motion's tribute poem. The England quintet from Wasps were made honorary burgesses of High Wycombe, and Lawrence Dallaglio joined with Jason Leonard and Joe Worsley in receiving the freedom of the Borough of Richmond. Not that anyone in that dignified Thamesside town was likely to impede the progress up and down the high street of those three substantial gentlemen.

Later on the day of his Campese outburst, Woodward was in much more benevolent mood as he hosted a black-tie dinner for the media at Lord's Cricket Ground. Reminders of great England days with bat and ball were to be seen in the museum opposite the Long Room – Ashes series wins and the like. England's rugby glory was in the here and now. The giant

An image of Martin Johnson holding the Webb Ellis Cup is projected onto a building on Circular Quay, Sydney.

scoreboard at the Nursery End flashed a warm golden message on that cold December evening: "England 20 Australia 17".

Woodward was very clear about when he wanted the partying to stop, and the hard work to start afresh. "I hope every single one of the players will cope with what is going on," he said, "especially the younger players who have got another World Cup to look forward to. They'll take it all in their stride and it will make them even more determined to get in the position to repeat the feat. We now know what it takes, and to see the reaction from the country makes the hard work from everyone, especially the players, really worthwhile. With the game against the New Zealand Barbarians out of the way, my mindset will change. On January 1, all of it will be history."

And that, neatly enough, coincided with the most prestigious set of awards of them all: the New Year's Honours List, a bonanza for the World Cup winners. Mindful of the way the 1966 football team had been almost completely overlooked, Tony Blair's government acted to avoid any repeat. Every player in the squad was decorated, either with an MBE, or in the cases of Wilkinson and Leonard, OBEs to go with their existing MBEs. Johnson, already an OBE after his captaincy of the 1997 Lions, was made a CBE. Andy Robinson, the forwards' coach, and Francis Baron, chief executive of the Rugby Football Union, were awarded OBEs; Phil Larder, Dave Reddin and Dave Alred from the support staff got MBEs. And Clive Woodward was knighted for services to rugby union. "It is a tribute to every member of the squad," Woodward said, "and the coaches, management and Zurich Premiership clubs who have all made a significant contribution to our success. The honours are richly deserved. I'd also like to thank my wife Jayne and my children for their fantastic support." Of the challenges to come, he said: "We've got to make all the right calls, and be very professional about what we do." It was not going to be as straightforward as he might have hoped...

"Jonny-mania"

The Premiership clubs, still getting to grips with the demands of the open game declared in 1995, had not always been uniformly supportive of England. But the chance to ride the crest of the wave of public interest was too good to miss, and the clubs set aside their wrangling over what they often saw as the intrusion of international rugby into their season. Sale supporters were given a website address to download photos of themselves taken with the Webb Ellis Cup. Gloucester reported ticket sales in their hundreds for the visit of Jonny Wilkinson's club, Newcastle Falcons, even though the match was two months away. In normal times, only the very keen or the very fastidious would book so long before the event. These were not normal times. This was the Wilkinson effect. Rugby followers old and new scanned the fixture list to see when the golden boy would be hitting their town. Schoolboys and girls, the lifeblood of England's future success, lined up on playing fields – at least, those that had survived being sold off as housing estates – to mimic Wilkinson's half-crouched kicking style, hands clasped out in front of him.

Sadly, the laws of public relations and physiology do not always make natural bedfellows. Wilkinson had hurt his shoulder making a tackle during the final against Australia; he also had a residual problem in the neck and shoulder region thought to date from his earliest playing days. It was the sort of ailment the man or woman in the street might have treated gradually with rest and rehabilitation. The man or woman in the street would not have put themselves in harm's way by tackling 15 stones of murderous Australian flanker.

Wilkinson's second domestic appearance of the 2003–04 season – the first had been against France at Twickenham before the World Cup – was eagerly anticipated. The question was when it would be. At the end of the day of the London victory parade, Wilkinson was involved in a car accident as a passenger on his way back to the northeast, which was said to be unconnected with his absence from his first possible outing with the Falcons, at home to Valladolid in the Parker Pen Challenge Cup. But there was an unsettlingly clinical nature to the medical bulletins that began to follow with the regularity of updates on the arrival of a royal baby. An initial release from the RFU said: "England and Newcastle fly-half Jonny Wilkinson had a CT scan of his neck today following discomfort this week. This showed a small healing fracture to the right facet joint at C5 in his neck. The injury is old and the scan shows damage to be relatively minor. The scan indicates a stable injury which, although it is not possible to identify exactly when it occurred, it is likely to have been at some time during the Rugby World Cup in Australia. Jonny's symptoms and neck examinations carried out by the England medical team during the World Cup did not suggest a significant problem at the time. As his discomfort settles, it is anticipated Jonny will be able to resume playing in two to three weeks' time."

Wilkinson was pencilled in for the Premiership match against Northampton on 28 December, and Newcastle could not print enough tickets at their recently renovated Kingston Park stadium. But it proved to be a sad and inappropriate footnote to the glory that had gone before. He kicked three penalties in the first half but a seemingly straightforward tackle left him crumpled in a heap for almost five minutes before he walked slowly from the field, cradling his arm, with more than a quarter of the match remaining. The verdict from Newcastle after an X-ray that evening referred to soft tissue damage and said Wilkinson might be back within "a few weeks". It turned out an operation was needed which would rule him out of the entire Six Nations Championship. He had the operation in mid-February and was released from hospital the following day. More weeks went by, and it was suggested he might be restored for Newcastle's Powergen Cup final at Twickenham in April, against Sale. No such luck. The hiatus continued, and England's tour to the southern hemisphere in June 2004 was rubbed out of the Wilkinson diary.

The unhappy chain of events did not deter some of the clubs' more resourceful PR people. Leeds hosted Newcastle at the end of March, and the Tykes thumped the tub of what they termed "Jonny-mania". They conceded that Wilkinson would not actually be playing, but the publicity blurb said: "The areas around the dug-out were the first to sell out, which shows that fans want to get as close as possible to the players... hoping to get a glimpse of Jonny and thank him for his efforts in Sydney." The glimpse was confined to the more eagle-eyed Leeds fans. Officially, Wilkinson was not at Headingley, although he did watch from the back of the stand.

His appearances were having to be rationed and stage-managed. He had won glowing praise from Wasps after playing at their ground in High Wycombe the previous Premiership season and, in the dark of a cold winter's evening, patiently signing autographs for a couple of hundred kids. It was a gentlemanly act but it belonged to pre-history. Wilkinson could not now just "turn up". At Newcastle home games he sometimes sought the seclusion of a hospitality box. Otherwise the world's greatest fly-half was restricted to acting as water-carrier to the team during matches. In this role, in front of a small end-of-season crowd at Rotherham, he was able to conduct an impromptu signing session for a few dozen lucky fans.

There was no shortage of non-rugby engagements. Everyone wanted to see, and be seen with, Jonny. Not many sports people have been accorded guest appearances on BBC's long-running *Parkinson* chat show – Muhammad Ali and Beckham spring to mind – but, clearly, the corporation had been forgiven for their Campese faux pas at the *Sports Review*. "Having watched *Parkinson* when growing up," said Wilkinson, "I felt privileged to be asked on. The other guests were Michael Portillo and Jeremy Clarkson and I chatted with them beforehand. I was nervous to begin with, but when I went on it felt like having a chat with someone in your own living-room."

Wilkinson was the official starter of the London Marathon alongside four-minute miler Roger Bannister, with Martin Johnson setting the wheelchair athletes away. Wilkinson's sponsors, Lucozade and Adidas, were prominent at the race, and these and other deals propelled him into *The Sunday Times*' Rich List, which quoted a personal fortune of £8m. The same weekend as the list was published, Wilkinson's contribution to Newcastle's Powergen Cup final win over Sale at Twickenham was restricted to ferrying drinks and instructions to and from the Falcons' players.

Wilkinson had, by choice, been used to living a quiet life, in a pleasant spot next to a golf course in Northumberland a few miles from Kingston Park. His parents, Phil and Philippa, moved from Surrey to Corbridge to be near him and his elder brother Mark, also a rugby player at Newcastle, and Jonny's closest confidant. Despite this close family support – Phil handles a lot of his son's business dealings – the signs of pressure showed towards the end of the season. A somewhat plaintive Wilkinson was interviewed on BBC Radio Five Live, discussing the effect on him of the World Cup. "People said that life would change," said Jonny, "and I thought that would mean more people would know who I was, and it would be a bit harder getting around town. But I didn't know – and I don't think those people knew – it would change in so many different areas and not all of them good. The simplicity of life has fallen away a bit. I've had to undergo quite a few tests in my character, some of which I've lost, you know, some of which I've kind of lost sight of. So I've had to do some rethinking and a bit of re-evaluating. I'm coming through it a better person but it's been tough." It made the World Cup sound more like a war than a rugby tournament. He was asked if it had altered his trust in the world. "It's split things in two," he said. "I've had some incredible responses, which have given me enormous pride and joy, and satisfaction. And also inspiration and motivation for carrying on, and for what direction my life goes in next. For example, I got

a letter from Elton Flatley [the Wallaby goal-kicker] after the final, which was wonderful, for someone to be so genuine in what must have been a soul-destroying defeat. I've had letters and experiences of meeting people, which have been just incredible. On the other hand you get the side of life which really tries to manipulate you in terms of what happened and that's where you divide: the people who use it as a positive experience and use it to spur their lives and help you in your life. And then those who try and make money out of your life, really, and try and manipulate you and in a way make your life worse and more difficult. That's been tough and I just try and stay on the right side of that line, really."

Martin Bayfield, the former England lock turned broadcaster and after-dinner speaker, predicted Wilkinson would deal with the challenge of fame. "He was the face, along with Martin Johnson, of England's World Cup victory, and the vultures have gathered around him… He'll get through it, and be stronger for it." While waiting to get back to doing what he liked best, Wilkinson went to work as an Ambassador for the NSPCC. Sculptor Nicholas Dimbleby produced 10 bronzes of Wilkinson's arms from the shoulder to the clasped hands, attached to a rugby ball, and the first was auctioned for St Thomas' Hospital's "Tommy's" baby charity. It went for £40,000. "Jonny-mania" certainly took many shapes and forms.

The Cup and Cheers
Meanwhile, the RFU, like the clubs, were busy capitalising on the lustrous appeal of the World Cup. They organised the "Sweet Chariot Tour" to take the Webb Ellis Cup (never "Bill", you will recall) to all corners of the country. Mike Tindall kicked off the tour by flying the trophy with Strike Command at 650mph to RAF Cosford. The pilot, Squadron Leader Simon Jessett of RAF Wittering, declared he was less nervous flying with Tindall than watching him play in the final against Australia. Three thousand people formed a parade of honour at Burton RFC, and the Ireland footballer Steve Staunton turned up with his son at Lichfield RFC – "It's the nearest we are going to get to a World Cup", Staunton joked. Cumbrian police fixed traffic lights on green and provided motorcycle escorts as 10,000 people saw the cup in 60 hours around the far northwest. Wilkinson was present on the Millennium Bridge in Newcastle-upon-Tyne for the handover of the cup from Northumberland to Durham, and he helped kids' teams play tag rugby in Bradford's Centenary Square. Instead of the normal chime at one the City Hall clock played the rugby anthem, "World in Union".

Francis Baron, chief executive of the RFU, escorted the cup into Lincoln Prison, and Jason Leonard and Martin Johnson got smiles of delight from sick children at Great Ormond Street and Coventry's Walsgrave Hospital. Completing a neat circle, the cup arrived back in London's Oxford Street in May, when Lewis Moody showed it off to West End shoppers once more. Possibly the youngest reveller in England's glory was Emily Maclean, born six hours after Wilkinson's winning dropped goal sailed over the bar in Sydney. Emily had her photo taken with the Cup in Leicester and her mum Nikki, a Leicester Tigers fan of course, said: "I was in labour on November the 22nd but I listened to the final. My husband went out and bought a radio."

Jonny Wilkinson looks bashful as he accepts his award for player of the year during the International Rugby Board awards at Wharf 8 in Sydney.

An England fan celebrates the victory long into the night at the Rocks in Sydney.

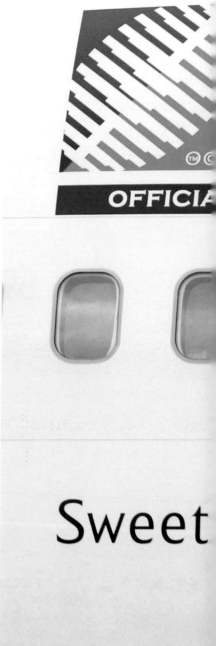

Above Clive Woodward waves to
fans as the England squad leave their
Manly hotel.

Right The England team on the steps
of the British Airways BA16 aircraft –
renamed "Sweet Chariot" – before
their departure from Sydney
International Airport.

Neil Back holds the cup high as crowds
of rugby fans welcome the England
team and the Webb Ellis Cup at
London's Heathrow Airport.

England hero Jonny Wilkinson is surrounded by police and fans as he makes his way through Heathrow Terminal 4.

Left Ross Hamilton, library officer at Twickenham's Museum of Rugby, places the Webb Ellis Cup in the trophy cabinet.

Above England head coach Clive Woodward, with his wife Jayne, outside Buckingham Palace holding his OBE, the forerunner to his knighthood.

Left On the day of the victory parade, England rugby fans await the arrival of the team in Trafalgar Square.

Right Clive Woodward celebrates as the open-topped bus inches towards Trafalgar Square.

Left Lawrence Dallaglio is all smiles as the team arrives in Trafalgar Square.

Above England players including Ben Cohen, Lewis Moody, Neil Back and Mike Tindall with a trophy-hugging Jason Leonard aboard the victory bus.

Left England captain Martin Johnson holds up the cup.

Above Fans took up every vantage point they could find.

Queen Elizabeth II poses with the victorious England rugby squad at a reception in Buckingham Palace.

Left Jonny Wilkinson with his girlfriend Diana Stuart after his MBE was awarded by Her Majesty the Queen at Buckingham Palace. After the World Cup this honour was upgraded to an OBE.

Above Jonny Wilkinson with the BBC Sports Personality of the Year award at Television Centre.

New prop Matt Stevens fends off New Zealand Barbarian Andrew Hore in the celebration match at Twickenham.

England fans celebrate a try against the New Zealand Baa-baas at Twickenham.

Left Martin Johnson holds the Webb Ellis Cup as he walks onto the field at Twickenham.

Above Jonny Wilkinson joins in the celebrations after the Barbarians game.

RBS
RBS

ENG

Towards
2007

Towards 2007

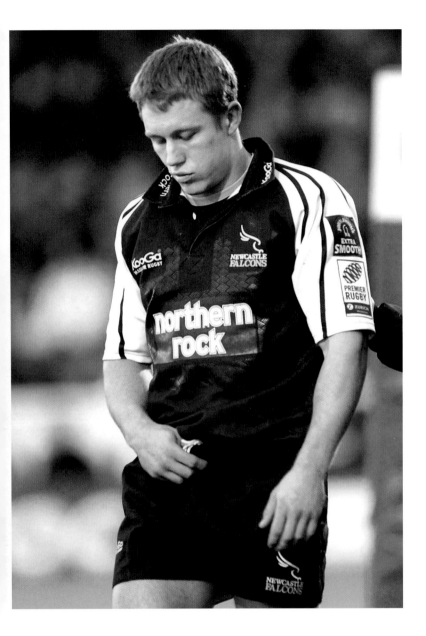

What happens when the cameras stop rolling and the flashbulbs cease popping? Steve Thompson, England's hooker throughout all 100 minutes of the World Cup final, admitted after getting home: "I can't remember ever feeling so depressed... It's a really weird experience. Maybe the reason for that was that at last we have come to the end of the road. I've been in this squad for two years now and, even though we always said we were travelling game by game, we always knew that the big prize was the World Cup." It was an entirely understandable reaction and, even though most of the squad were thrust straight back into playing for their clubs, it was always likely to be difficult to contemplate setting out on another road with England, in the Six Nations Championship.

Sir Clive Woodward, who briefly had to deny a bizarre link with the vacant role of Springbok coach, said: "We've beaten the bad guys [of the southern hemisphere] 12 times in a row, and won the World Cup. If you'd said that in 1997, people would have thought you were mad." Now, however, there was another lot of "bad guys" closer to home to contend with. "You can't stand still", said Woodward. "You've got to bring in one or two new people, and that's what I'm planning to do. It's a brutal business and I'm very clear about that. If we take our foot off the pedal, and have a string of losses, there'll be changes, and I include myself in that. The next World Cup's a long way away, and I think we're going to see one of the best Six Nations' of all time, because you've got the world champions playing."

But the world champions would have to play without their towering totem, Martin Johnson. At the age of 33, the one-time bank worker departed the Test scene with an unparalleled swag bag of trophies as a winning skipper: a World Cup, Lions' tour (1997), Grand Slam, Triple Crown, Six Nations title, Calcutta Cup (against Scotland) and Cook Cup (against Australia). Johnson intended to carry on playing for at least another season with his club, Leicester, having led them additionally to the Heineken Cup twice and the domestic league and cup. "I think I probably knew in my heart that I wouldn't be playing for England again," he said of his feelings at the World Cup final. Unlike Maria Callas, who tried to sing on when her voice had gone, "Johno" knew when it was time to go.

Before the 2003–04 season was out, five more of the World Cup squad – Kyran Bracken, Jason Leonard, Neil Back, Dorian West and Paul Grayson – would follow. They all chose their moment in different ways, but together with injuries such as that to Wilkinson and the sense of anti-climax articulated by Thompson, this was an obvious watershed in the Woodward era. Needless to say, the coach tackled the situation head-on: Leonard and Back began the Six Nations in February declaring themselves available for England selection as normal. Neither made it through to the end, against France in late March. For these two stalwarts – almost 200 caps between them – and for Woodward's squad as a whole, it was a spring of surprises.

New for Old – Italy and Scotland

The references to 1966 and all that were dusted down again, for wasn't it Scotland who had been the first to defeat Alf Ramsey's World Cup winners,

New England captain Lawrence Dallaglio (third from the left) at the launch in London of the 2004 Six Nations Championship with (left to right) Italy's captain Andrea de Rossi, Scotland squad member Gordon Bulloch, France squad member Olivier Brouzet, Ireland captain Brian O'Driscoll and Wales captain Colin Charvis.

at Wembley in 1967? During the Six Nations, the annual jamboree that predates rugby's World Cup by more than 100 years, the Scots would be joined by the Italians, Welsh, Irish and French in taking a tilt at England's world champion windmill.

All the talk in Italy on Valentine's weekend was of absent friends. Brian "The Pitbull" Moore, a former England hooker turned television commentator, said of Johnson: "Captains and forwards can be replaced, but as a man, he was the one who dragged everything together when it started to go pear-shaped." The new captain was in fact an old captain. Woodward had turned again to Lawrence Dallaglio, who lost the job in 1999 after a tabloid newspaper imbroglio. For the Italian-descended skipper, it was doubly poignant. The first post-World Cup Test selection contained 10 members of the team from the final, with Jason Robinson shifted to inside centre alongside Will Greenwood, a position he was familiar with from Sale, but had only dallied with for England. In Wilkinson's place at fly-half, Woodward preferred the experience of Grayson to 22-year-old Cornishman Olly Barkley, a multi-talented sportsman who had been progressing nicely at his club, Bath, since winning a first cap in North America in 2001. Wasps' Alex King remained on the periphery while Charlie Hodgson was again out of the picture, having suffered a fresh knee injury with Sale.

The principal cause of raised eyebrows was the absence from the 28-man preparatory squad, never mind the final 22, of Neil Back. Clearly, Woodward was not going to select on reputation alone. Back had been captain when Johnson was injured the last time England went to Rome in 2002. He was in charge of defence during the World Cup. Now, Back was said to have paid the price for indifferent form with his club, Leicester. Two other Tigers forwards, Martin Corry and Graham Rowntree, were also surplus to England's requirements.

Not that Woodward threw the baby out with the bath water. This was only the start of the long process of dovetailing the survivors of 2003 with the country's burgeoning young talent to defend the World Cup at the next finals in France in 2007. Barkley was joined on the bench by Sale's Chris Jones, a 23-year-old beanpole of a back rower blessed with raw pace. These two, together with James Simpson-Daniel, the versatile Gloucester back, and Bath lock Steve Borthwick, formed the vanguard of England's new wave in the Six Nations. But several others who had enjoyed a glimpse of the limelight against the New Zealand Barbarians – the likes of Ollie Smith, Stuart Abbott, Andy Titterrell, Matt Stevens, Andy Sheridan, Hugh Vyvyan and Pat Sanderson – would have to wait a little longer for their turn. Three young wings of great promise – Marcel Garvey, Ugo Monye and Richard Haughton – continued to make their way with the England Under-21 and Sevens sides.

Johnson was in Rome, but as a fan not a player. Indeed, he had brought his wife out for the occasion. Among the rest of England's followers it was Sydney revisited, friends reunited. Out came the silly wigs and jester hats. The raucous singing of "God Save the Queen" was, as usual, several beats ahead of the marching band. The difference was that the flags of St George were newly adorned with the legend "World Champions". The BBC

commentators pointed out that Grayson had never started a Six Nations game. It was mere pedantry – he had started a dozen Five Nations matches before Italy joined the party in 2000, and before Wilkinson took over. In the England years BC – Before Clive – Grayson was accustomed to a "let's not lose" mentality. Under Woodward, he now reflected, performance was the thing, and winning the only aim.

Italy selected a new scrum-half, the dreadlocked Paul Griffen, and a rangy pack who were energetic but ultimately limited. England had averaged 50 points in winning all nine previous meetings, and maintained the record to a tee. They scored seven tries, including four which originated at the line-out, a statistic both Andy Robinson and future Six Nations opponents would have noted with interest. Two tries came from counter-attacks, and the seventh and last was made by Matt Dawson, on as a substitute for Andy Gomarsall, harrying Griffen behind a scrum and prompting Chris Jones, on the field for Joe Worsley, to break sharply off the flank for a debut try. Barkley, given 10 minutes or so to sample Six Nations life for the first time, missed the conversion.

Italy broke England's defensive line four times but bemoaned their inability to convert the positions into tries. After an opening drop goal by Griffen's fellow New Zealander, Rima Wakarua, England settled to their task with a try by Iain Balshaw. A line-out, two rucks and a feint from Robinson to fix the defenders sent the blond flyer through. Next to score was Robinson himself, who fielded a kick and exchanged passes with Josh Lewsey before executing a trademark mid-air step, like a rugby-playing Rudolf Nureyev, to leave Wakarua clutching thin air and bowing his head at missing the tackle. Robinson went over twice more, either side of half-time, to complete a hat-trick, notwithstanding the inconvenience somewhere in between of ripping the nail off a middle finger. Grayson collected his own chip over the defence – albeit one that appeared meant for Robinson's temporary replacement, Henry Paul – to make it 45–9. Dusk had fallen when Jones pounced to bring up the half-century. Italy's full-back, Andrea Masi, was a menace but sadly he was never fully fit for the rest of the Championship, which went on to produce defeats by France, Ireland and Wales, and a morale-raising win over Scotland in Rome. The teetotaller Robinson left the Eternal City with a bottle of man-of-the-match champagne. "I'm allowed one glass," he insisted. Asked to assess the team's performance, Robinson said: "We'll wait until Monday and look at the video." Such is the caution of the modern sportsman.

If Scotland were going to get any change out of England a week later at Murrayfield, they would need to attack the world champions' line-out and take it from there. This indeed was one of the few areas of strength available to the Scots, whose first match under their new coach, Matt Williams, had been a dispiriting defeat by Wales in Cardiff. Recognising the threat, England adjusted their starting line-up to include Jones among a gargantuan quartet of line-out targets with Danny Grewcock, Ben Kay and Dallaglio. Grewcock had partnered Martin Johnson many times in England's second row, jumping in the middle of the line-out as a result. Now, with Johnson gone, he could take up his preferred position at the front.

It was an early evening kick-off in Edinburgh. Rugby's popularity prompted the BBC to tap into a family audience settling down for their normal Saturday diet of dating shows, quizzes and lottery draws. Murrayfield's pre-match entertainment was a firework-laden spectacular of sound and vision, a preamble of a kind often seen at Twickenham, but Woodward complained: "It's a sports event, not a pop concert." Dallaglio led his team out straight into a forest of bandsmen. Once the England captain had untangled himself from the bagpipes he introduced his players to the Princess Royal. Jason Leonard, as one of the substitutes, was at the end of the line. It proved to be appropriate. The great man of Harlequins did not get on, and when he was left out of the 22 for the following match against Ireland in favour of Matt Stevens it was the signal for him to give up all together. It had been a career beyond the reach of superlatives: 114 England caps, and five more for the Lions, was a world record, and utterly remarkable given the demands of his position in the front row. Equally important were the sportsmanship and sense of proportion for which Leonard was famous throughout the game. Leonard's final bow would come in May with victory for his club in the Parker Pen Challenge Cup, and a try-scoring appearance for the Barbarians at Twickenham. He will never be forgotten wherever rugby union is discussed and held dear.

Returning to Murrayfield, when the action finally got under way, England's first line-out throw went astray but they were solid in that department thereafter. It was, though, a strange match. England won 35–13, scoring four tries to one, without producing a convincing performance. Their first three tries each had an element of fortune or Scottish complicity about them, or both. The white jerseys were more efficient in defence than in Rome, and a rare lapse came when Iain Balshaw was caught on the hop by a wicked bounce as his Bath club-mate Simon Danielli chipped ahead and pouched the ball for Scotland's try in the 57th minute.

The experiment with Robinson at centre continued, and the convert popped up as first receiver in the opening stages. After Chris Paterson's penalty gave Scotland a 3–0 lead, Robinson found himself in almost an identical position to the one which brought England's first try in Italy. This time he chipped over the Scots instead of passing, Ben Hinshelwood slipped in attempting to cover and Ben Cohen dashed past the floundering Scotland full-back to score. Grayson converted and then added a penalty. At close quarters, England were stronger in ruck and maul. It seems the days are over when Scotland can whistle up horny-handed sons of the soil to repel the English with brawn alone. In the loose, though, Jason White and Tom Philip tackled hard.

Scotland should have had a try after 20 minutes, when Chris Cusiter fished the ball from a pond of confetti and Paterson sent Danielli through. Robinson missed the tackle on his left shoulder, but Danielli spilled possession with the line beckoning. Paterson and Grayson exchanged penalties, the latter when Philip conceded a blatant penalty at a ruck. "Right in at the side," screamed the ever-enthusiastic Woodward; Andy Robinson and Phil Larder wore looks that said 'er, yes, we know'. England's second try also sprang from the boot of Robinson. Danielli collected a long punt but

A wax figure of Jonny Wilkinson is unveiled in at Madame Tussauds in London. Visitors are taught by a rugby coach how to emulate Wilkinson's unique preparation ritual and trademark hand clasp before taking place kicks.

was charged down by the elastically-limbed Jones. Trevor Woodman and Grewcock took it up, surviving a Scottish shout for a knock-on, and Balshaw muscled past the stumbling Cusiter to get the ball down. Grayson's conversion put England ahead 20–6 at half-time.

Scotland were keen to kick deep and wide, and it might have paid dividends had they been more accurate. Six minutes into the second half, England got lucky again when a miscued pass from Gomarsall behind a line-out was turned into a good one by Greenwood, who chipped ahead for Paterson to be charged down by Josh Lewsey for another try. Though Danielli struck back to make it 25–13, England coasted to victory. Simon Taylor went to the sin-bin, the seven-man Scotland scrum was rudely shoved to one side and Grewcock's knee-pumping run after Dallaglio's initial break was irresistible. The highlight of a quiet last 14 minutes was Jones, who could be well satisfied with his full debut, almost getting a try from a diagonal kick by Grayson.

Dallaglio collected the Calcutta Cup after the 121st recurrence of rugby's oldest international fixture, and said: "I've been very pleased with our physicality in the last two games. What we need to add to that now is to possibly think a bit more about the way we are playing and, when we create opportunities, be aware of how to finish them off."

Back Home for Ireland and Wales

Twickenham sometimes throws open its gates to allow corporate customers and rugby enthusiasts the chance to peek inside the changing rooms where England prepare to perform. There are golden plaques lining the walls, recalling past victories, and a little wooden notice board where the best attacking and defensive players from the previous fixture have their names posted up. Each player has a cubicle to himself, with a weights room and practice area just around the corner. The visitor is left to imagine what nerves and anticipation must fill these corridors when 75,000 spectators await at the end of the tunnel. Reserve scrum-half Andy Gomarsall summed it up: "That's why we do all the hard work. Whenever I run out at Twickenham, I say to myself that's why I do it. The game is as much mental as physical. Remembering those feelings fuels you to work harder and train harder."

After England's two wins on the road, HQ was ready for the first proper Test since the World Cup. The familiar cast was present and correct: barbour-wearers and ticket touts, flag-sellers and company directors, businessmen and bog attendants. Twickenham on a match day is Royal Ascot, FA Cup Final and Walthamstow dogs rolled into one. It has always been difficult to get a ticket. Now more than ever, everyone wanted a piece of the world champions. And that, of course, included their next opponents, Ireland.

Consider the record. In the previous four years England had played 49 Tests home and away, winning 44 of them at an average cost of fewer than 13 points conceded per match. They had captured a world title, a Grand Slam and three Six Nations Championships. At Twickenham, the story was even more compelling. The All Blacks were the last to upset the picnic hampers in the West Car Park, during the 1999 World Cup. Since then, 22 teams of

Back to training – the England team are shown the way by the new captain Lawrence Dallaglio.

varying quality, from Wallabies to Springboks to Romanians had tried and failed as England set up a world record run for a home team in Tests.

Ireland arrived on the back of a solid display in defeat in France, and a comfortable win over Wales in Dublin. Apart from the injured Leicester wing, Geordan Murphy, they were at full strength and in good heart. As ever, primary possession at scrum and line-out held the key. England had lost the unfortunate Grewcock to an Achilles' tendon injury, Simon Shaw was also unavailable, so in came the sure-handling but less physical Steve Borthwick. Ireland had Paul O'Connell and Malcolm O'Kelly, two of the world's most effective line-out operators on their day. It proved to be one of those days.

Any hooker worth his salt will testify that the line-out is a fiendish combination of physical and mental checks and balances, with many potential pitfalls. But there was no denying that Thompson had a stinker throwing in. England lost 11 of their throws. Any team would struggle to offset such a deficit, even the world champions. It seemed England would avert disaster early in the second quarter when Matt Dawson upset opposite number Peter Stringer at a scrum, Richard Hill poked the ball upfield and Paul Grayson fed Dawson to score behind the posts. Grayson converted and soon after knocked over a penalty awarded at a scrum to make it 10–6 to England. But Ronan O'Gara, Ireland's fly-half, recovered from an initial miss to kick four penalties and give Ireland a 12–10 half-time lead. O'Gara went against the grain of conventional wisdom by saying that England missed Wilkinson more than Johnson. "The mood our forwards were in," O'Gara said, "I don't think they'd have cared who they were up against."

The pivotal moment came 10 minutes into the second half. Gordon D'Arcy, one of the revelations of the Championship alongside Brian O'Driscoll in Ireland's midfield, shook off Will Greenwood, and O'Kelly almost scored at the right-hand corner. Ireland kept going, and superb long passes by their centres ushered Girvan Dempsey over on the opposite wing. O'Gara added the extras and England trailed by two scores. Ben Cohen and Mark Regan, on for Thompson, went close to a try; Grayson kicked another penalty. Ireland won 19–13. The home record was gone, and with it the cloak of invincibility draped over the world champions' shoulders. "My sweetest day on a rugby field," said Reg Corrigan, the Ireland prop. Those who had been angered by the rejigging of the Six Nations fixtures to pit England against France on the final day nodded in agreement.

England had, by and large, accepted World Cup glory with grace and humility. The reaction to this defeat needed to be in the same vein. "Ireland thoroughly deserved to win," said Josh Lewsey. "Our failure in the set-piece has been highlighted, but the sign of a good side is to stick together – and I know there is no blame culture and no back-stabbing among this squad. As we shared the good times together, we will carry the responsibility of failure as a squad. Our unbeaten record [at Twickenham] had to end at some stage and in many ways it was positive this extra pressure has been lifted."

The upshot was the end for the time being of the Jason Robinson experiment, a call-up to fly-half for Olly Barkley and a clear-the-air meeting among the players at Twickenham on the Monday before the Wales match. "They made some errors but it's been fixed quickly," said Sir Clive. The press wanted to pin the coach down on what precisely was being done in training, but Woodward's body swerve to an unwanted question is usually as effective metaphorically as it was physically in his playing career. "It's not about what happens in training," he said. "It's about what happens at four o'clock next Saturday afternoon. We know why we lost. I believe you'll see a different performance."

A temporary distraction was a mini-scandal surrounding the allocation of match tickets to the players. Tickets belonging to Ben Cohen, Matt Stevens and Olly Barkley had found their way into the wrong hands. The RFU had already acted to head off a black market which had mushroomed from a cottage industry of touts on street corners to a six-figure business at every Twickenham event. In the process the Union were accused of, effectively, bringing the black market in-house: three hospitality firms were licensed to buy tickets from clubs at whatever price they saw fit. The RFU's commercial boss, Paul Vaughan, argued: "We police the system heavily and we estimate that 2,000 tickets out of 75,000 still go onto the black market. We are actively investigating how 200 tickets for the Ireland and Wales games ended up where they did. For at least four games a year, we could sell out the stadium four or five times over."

With Wales and France to come, it was time for Back and Leonard to go. Unlike Johnson, who staged an orderly press conference after a Heineken Cup match at Leicester, Back's announcement might have been handled better. The flanker raged in a tabloid newspaper column about being left on the bench while things went awry against Ireland. Woodward showed his tough side, stating implacably: "One day he [Back] will be a coach, sitting here. I've probably given Neil Back 99 per cent of good news, so he's got to cop the bad news when it comes. I'm not here to look after people's retirement parties." A quieter departure was Louise Ramsay's from the role of team manager, to be replaced by Abigail Findlay, a former head of sales for London Irish and Harlequins. Meanwhile, the train leaving Platform One had Jason Leonard's name on it – seeking positive publicity, for once, an engine for the railway company C2C was branded in Leonard's honour for use on the Southend line in his native Essex.

Wales came to Twickenham with a scrum that had misfired badly against France in their previous match, a defeat in Cardiff, but a set of backs continuing to play the expansive stuff that helped light up the World Cup. England had Mike Tindall and Grewcock back from injury. Hill, who operated throughout the Championship at openside flanker, had Chris Jones back alongside him in place of Joe Worsley. Barkley began by missing a tackle on Wales's Tom Shanklin but recovered to exert a notable influence on the match. Still, England had to fight all the way for their 31–21 win.

Cohen scored after five minutes, with Barkley committing his opposing No. 10, Stephen Jones, to a tackle, and Grewcock energetically supporting the move on the far side of a ruck. Barkley converted, then Stephen Jones landed two penalties for 7–6. A capricious breeze did not deter the kickers. Bursts of pop music, de rigueur at the modern Twickenham, greeted each successful attempt as Barkley and Jones took the scoreline to 16–9.

Martin Johnson, summarising for television at half-time, said: "I think there's tries out there for them." But he meant England, not Wales. Eighty-four seconds into the second half, Twickenham sensed a repeat of the Ireland defeat. A couple of long cut-out passes put Gareth Thomas over for a record-equalling 33rd Test try for Wales. Perhaps England were surprised that Wales had taken a clean line-out, for the visitors were no Ireland in that regard. Captain Dallaglio read the riot act under the posts as Stephen Jones converted. Fortunately for England, the Llanelli man missed his next two attempts, a penalty and the conversion of a second thrilling try to the wide by Mark Taylor, otherwise Wales might have led by more than 21–16. The barbour brigade were reaching for their hip flasks when even Gareth Llewellyn, Wales's 35-year-old replacement lock, found a gap in England's defence.

But Dallaglio's leadership was not to be underestimated. The No. 8 drove hard around the fringes, and rallied those around him. Twickenham went potty when Cohen reached beyond Dwayne Peel and Jonathan Thomas to dot down his 28th try in 39 Tests. Cleverly, Cohen gestured to Thomas to step back behind the hindmost foot of his team-mates at the ruck before plunging into the resulting space. Barkley converted and England had a good last quarter. A sweet set-move, with Cohen in support of Greenwood, then Dawson flipping a reverse pass to Ben Kay, ended with a ruck penalty that Barkley kicked to make it 26–21. With two minutes remaining, Dallaglio picked up at a scrum, Dawson ducked blind and Cohen sent replacement Worsley in. Barkley's conversion miss was his first of the match but at that stage it did not matter. "It was good to be back in the saddle," said Tindall. "I feel fit and I am looking forward to a tough challenge against France." Overnight England were top of the Six Nations table, but the French took over again with a straightforward Sunday win in Scotland.

Passion in Paris

The Championship's seven-week format allowed little opportunity to take stock. And the confusion – some would say obfuscation – during the World Cup regarding the injury to Richard Hill reared its ugly head again with an extraordinary about-turn between Monday and Tuesday of the most important week of England's Six Nations' season. These were the headlines on successive days in *The Times*: "Grayson's experience proves the key", followed by "Barkley eager for French test". On the Monday, Grayson said: "I am 100 per cent fit… it is nice to know that being a veteran can get you in a side as well as keep you out." The following day he was declared unfit, and Barkley returned, ahead of Mike Catt by dint of his more reliable goal-kicking.

The Triple Crown and Grand Slam were already out of reach, but a win in Paris would enable England to retain their Six Nations' title and allow Lawrence Dallaglio to lift the trophy for the first time in his two stints as captain. His team were learning to cope with being second favourites again. Changes in personnel had affected their substance, but what about the style? "Circumstances change," reasoned Ben Cohen. "We're world champions, and we're enjoying the feeling of being world champions. At the same time, our opponents are enjoying taking big shots at us. If everyone played the same way all the time, rugby would be one bloody boring sport."

It was part of a fascinating debate over rugby's fundamentals: how much had the loss of a couple of individuals affected the team as a whole? How much of a contribution do the frailties and strengths of human beings make – their emotions, rational thought and irrational behaviour – and to what extent can a coach or captain control them? Never mind the length of a piece of string. How long does it take to create a winning team, and how long might it take to unravel one? Will Greenwood was another to tackle head-on the question of whether England's backs were underperforming, or forever doomed to unfavourable comparison with some rose-tinted memory of previous efforts. "What we became really good at over a period of years," said Greenwood, "was not just wearing down our opponents, but keeping them down. Recently, we've been guilty of letting teams back into games. It's not a case of us misfiring in the backs, it's a case of failing to maintain the pressure we're creating." These were the topics of conversation as England's supporters made their much-loved biennial trip to Paris. Flooding the boulevards and the bars, they were a little put out at having to wait for kick-off at 9pm on a Saturday evening, another development led by television. Very few would get home that night, but the rich anticipation of the World Cup semi-final rematch made it worthwhile.

France were playing for a Grand Slam – their fourth in eight years – but England could take the Championship if they won by seven points and maintained a superior try count overall. "I would take a one-point victory, to be honest," said Joe Worsley, recalled for the injured Chris Jones. England ran out first, followed by Fabien Pelous, France's captain in succession to Fabien Galthié, amid a burst of Europop that made the stadium shake. Then, a calming interlude, with the band playing "Ode to Joy", anthem of the European Union but, funnily enough, not a tune often heard at Twickenham before a match…

France fell offside in the first minute, and Dallaglio tangled with his opposing No. 8, Imanol Harinordoquy – dubbed by some "Harry Ordinary" after the World Cup encounter. Olly Barkley missed the penalty, though his studied kicking routine made Jonny Wilkinson's look slapdash. Olivier Magne led a French break but made the mistake of taking the long route around Phil Vickery – the prop slammed his opponent back with a ferocious tackle. It added up to an exciting start and, England, mauling a line-out 20 metres upfield, were in good nick. Then the French front row drove their counterparts up at a scrum, and Dimitri Yachvili, the scrum-half, kicked a penalty for 3–0. Danny Grewcock twisted an ankle and was replaced by Steve Borthwick. From the next line-out, Yachvili kicked diagonally to find Harinordoquy in loads of space. The Basque back rower waited for the bounce, which was kind, and made the try. Two more penalties from Yachvili followed. With 35 minutes gone it was 14–0. Barkley put over a penalty when Pascal Papé went over the top of a ruck but the restart brought more trouble. The ball flew over Ben Kay's head, France gathered in and, with Matt Dawson grounded at the ruck, Yachvili darted round the short side, chipped ahead and scored a few metres infield from the left corner. The No. 9 was defying absolutely his reputation as a possible weak link, and added the conversion for good measure.

Clive Woodward and Andy Robinson had a new set of challenges looking ahead to 2007.

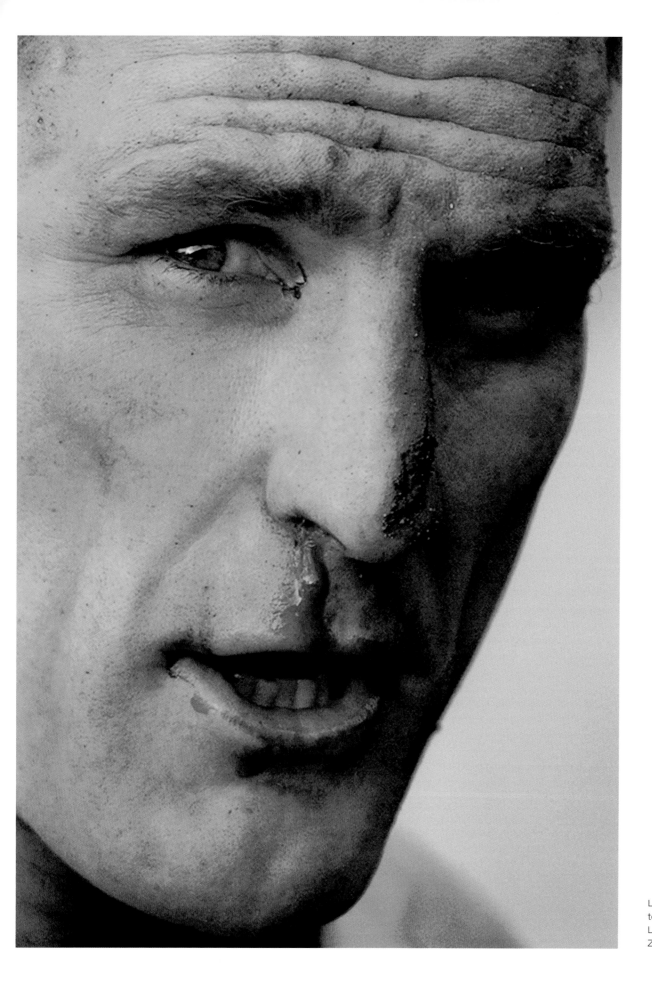

Lawrence Dallaglio shows the signs of a tough game as he is interviewed after London Wasps took on Bath in the Zurich Premiership.

Dallaglio had said beforehand: "We have got a rebuilding process and I knew it was going to be a very tough job. I also knew that whatever we did would be compared to what we had done, and whatever I did as captain would be compared to Martin Johnson. But we've got to create our own identity and if that means taking a couple of steps back initially in order to go forward, then that's what's going to happen." The bold reaction from England, trailing 21–3 at half-time, offered encouragement for the future. Barkley kicked a penalty and though an English hand in the ruck allowed Yachvili to make it 24–6 in the 51st minute, these were France's last points of the evening. In another tit-for-tat score, England poured forward, Borthwick won a turnover at a ruck and Mike Catt, on for Greenwood, lobbed a pass out to put Cohen in on the left. Catt, like Dallaglio perhaps, might not be around for 2007, but here, as in the World Cup, his calm assurance was a delight to watch.

The French gloried in the extraordinary statistic that they won 16 pieces of possession in their opponents' 22, to one by England, but the white jerseys kept coming. With 10 minutes left, a line-out penalty was dispatched by Barkley. Next Kay won a line-out on the England 10-metre line, Barkley kicked to Nicolas Brusque, who was tackled by Tindall, and Kay tackled Christophe Dominici. England attacked through Julian White, and Dawson, Catt, Tindall and Barkley combined for Josh Lewsey to cut inside Dominici and hand off Frédéric Michalak for a fine try. Barkley's conversion cut the French lead to 24–21. It seemed France might make a similar misjudgement to Australia's in the last knockings of the World Cup final. With time up, they ran the ball instead of booting it dead, and Jason Robinson had one last rousing dash of the season. But it came to nothing. The final whistle brought forth French joy and Pelous to receive the Six Nations trophy. England went into a huddle, with Sir Clive Woodward joining them for a moment, then stood and applauded their conquerors. Pelous and Magne, in achieving their fourth Grand Slams, joined an exclusive and hitherto all-English band comprising Jason Leonard, and three men from the early part of the 20th century, Cyril Lowe, Willie Davies and Ronnie Cove-Smith.

From Gold to Bronze

England had lost two matches, and finished third in the Six Nations for the first time since 1993. But in retreat they could reflect on some compliments paid to them, back-handed or otherwise. The Yachvili cross-kick had been a favourite tactic in England for several years. The defensive coaches of the two teams who beat the world champions were both English: Mike Ford for Ireland, and Dave Ellis for France. And Bernard Laporte, France's coach, said: "When you win against the best in the world, you have to be happy. I think England are the best team in the world." The unshakeable English sense of humour – self-deprecating, wry, sardonic – summed it up best when *Private Eye* magazine carried an "apology": "We wish to apologise for conveying the impression that England had a world-beating team of superheroes. We now recognise that they are, in fact, a bunch of overweight middle-aged has-beens. We are sorry for any false impression that may have been given."

After Paris, the players went for the usual post-match meal, which also happened to be post-midnight. The speeches dragged on, and dinner was finally done at about 3am. As Josh Lewsey put it: "Even the French struggled with the lamb shank at a time more usually reserved for kebabs." But Woodward was up early the following morning. In fact, when he met the bleary-eyed members of the press at 8.15 the word soon went round that he had watched the video tape of the match in the wee small hours and, in fact, had not slept at all. "We are going through a bit of change," Woodward said. "You don't like it, but you have to coach and play your way through it. You can't be afraid of losing, especially with new players. They've got to know what it's all about. I'm proud of the side, and we'll take a lot out of the second half, but this sport is about winning, and we have lost." Steve Thompson was interviewed on BBC Radio Five Live on the Monday evening for a Six Nations summing-up. "We played an hour of good rugby in the whole Championship," said the unhappy hooker. "The last 20 minutes against Wales, and the second half against France."

A team of the tournament appeared in the French daily sports newspaper, *L'Equipe*, and only Ben Cohen from England made it in, compared with eight players in the 2003 version. There were nine Frenchmen, including six in the pack, four from Ireland and one from Wales. Italy and Scotland had none. Happily, the wider world was not yet ready to forget Sydney. Rugby World Cup Ltd announced in early April a surplus of £64.3 million, a 36 per cent increase on the return from 1999. Gate receipts at the 2003 tournament topped £1.9 million while the global television audience was put at 3.4 billion. In May, England were named World Team of the Year at the Laureus World Sports Awards in Estoril, Portugal. Suited and booted, Martin Johnson, Neil Back and Ben Kay were on hand to collect the prize. Other contenders were football's AC Milan, the Australian cricket team, Ferrari, the Alinghi America's Cup sailing team and the German women's football team. Jonny Wilkinson was nominated as Sportsman of the Year, but was edged out by the Formula One world champion, Michael Schumacher. Woodward collected Sport England's Coach of the Year award in London; he was also appointed head coach to the British & Irish Lions for the tour to New Zealand in 2005. "I could have stood down after the World Cup and got on to the motivational-speaking circuit," said Woodward, "but that's not for me. I want to move the England team on to new and even better challenges. As other countries chase us we've got to move forward. I want to see if we can win a World Cup and play well at the same time."

To borrow from Kipling, in 2003, England won the World Cup, and theirs was the earth, and everything that's in it. They talked with crowds and kept their virtue; they walked with a Queen but did not lose the common touch. In 2004 they met with triumph's twin impostor and kept their heads while others about them were losing theirs. Until 2007, they and only they can be called England: Rugby World Champions. If that's all they have, it surely is enough.

Above Martin Johnson announces his retirement from international rugby after playing for his club Leicester Tigers against Ulster.

Right Lawrence Dallaglio at the British Museum for the launch of the 2004 Six Nations Championship.

Left A proud moment for Italian-descended Lawrence Dallaglio as he sings the national anthem before the Six Nations match against Italy at the Flaminio Stadium in Rome.

Above Italian players during their national anthem.

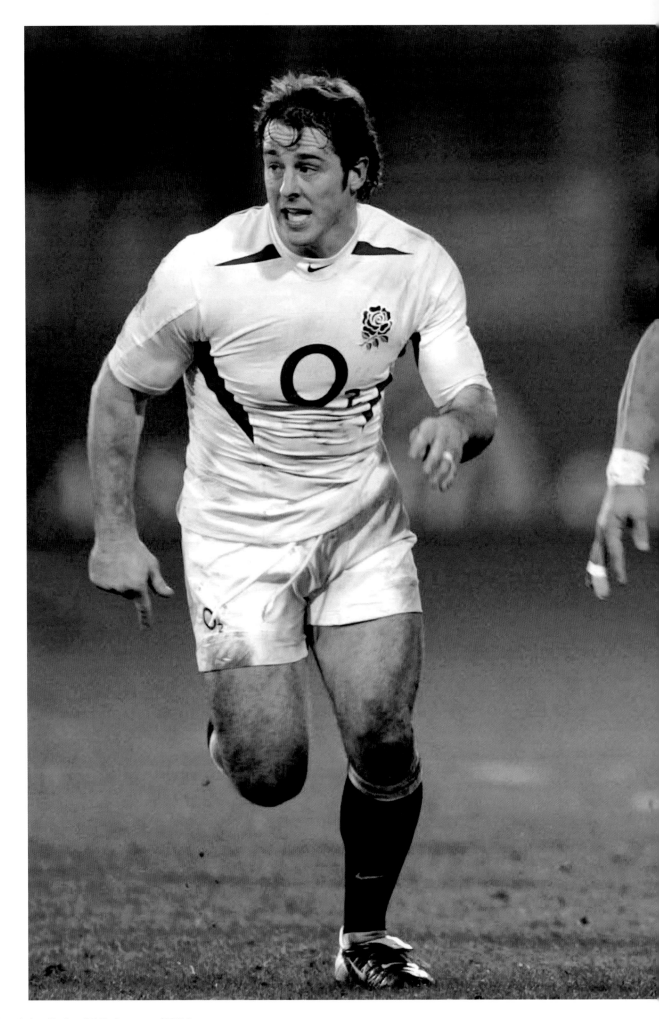

Jason Robinson, scorer of three tries against Italy, makes a break with support from Andy Gomarsall and Ben Cohen.

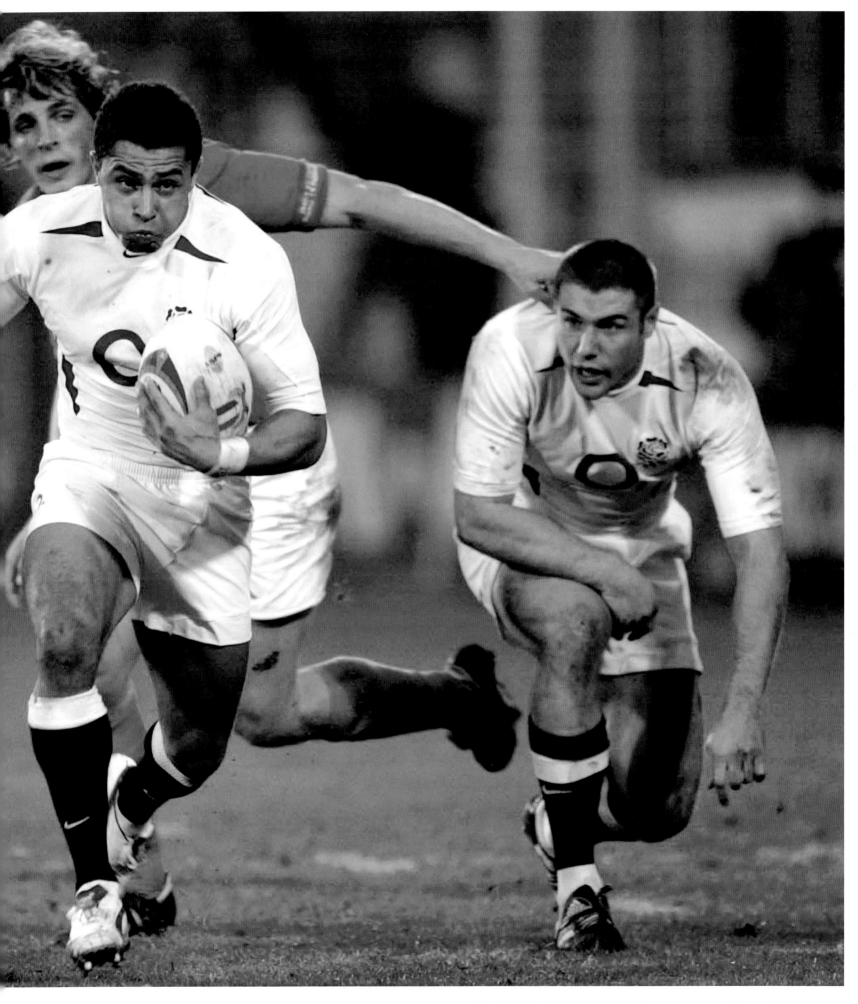

Above Replacement England scrum-half Matt Dawson is held by Paul Griffen of Italy.

Right Josh Lewsey is caught by Denis Dallan of Italy.

Left Sir Clive Woodward back at Pennyhill Park.

Right Chris Jones (right), one of the new guard of England players, joins Richard Hill in training at Bagshot.

Above Ben Cohen celebrates with Will Greenwood after Cohen scored the opening try against Scotland.

Right Scottish optimism was quickly snuffed out by dominant England at Murrayfield.

Above Scotland's Simon Webster is upended by Ben Cohen at Murrayfield.

Right Danny Grewcock dives over the line to score England's fourth try against the Scots.

A new-look back row of Lawrence Dallaglio, Chris Jones and Richard Hill pose with the Calcutta Cup after the 35–13 defeat of Scotland.

Previous pages England players stretch during another training session at Pennyhill Park.

Above England fan Chris Munton enjoys a drink before the Six Nations match against Ireland at Twickenham.

Right An England fan gets in her seat early before the Ireland game.

Jason Robinson is sent sprawling by an ankle tap tackle from Ireland's scrum-half Peter Stringer.

Above Sir Clive Woodward feels the pressure during the match with Ireland.

Right Ireland captain Brian O'Driscoll takes off after kicking downfield.

Above Will Greenwood goes close to scoring a try in the last few minutes of the Ireland match.

Right Ronan O'Gara and Kevin Maggs celebrate after the final whistle as Lawrence Dallaglio appears stunned. Ireland won 19–13.

Lawrence Dallaglio stretches at
Pennyhill Park before the match
with Wales.

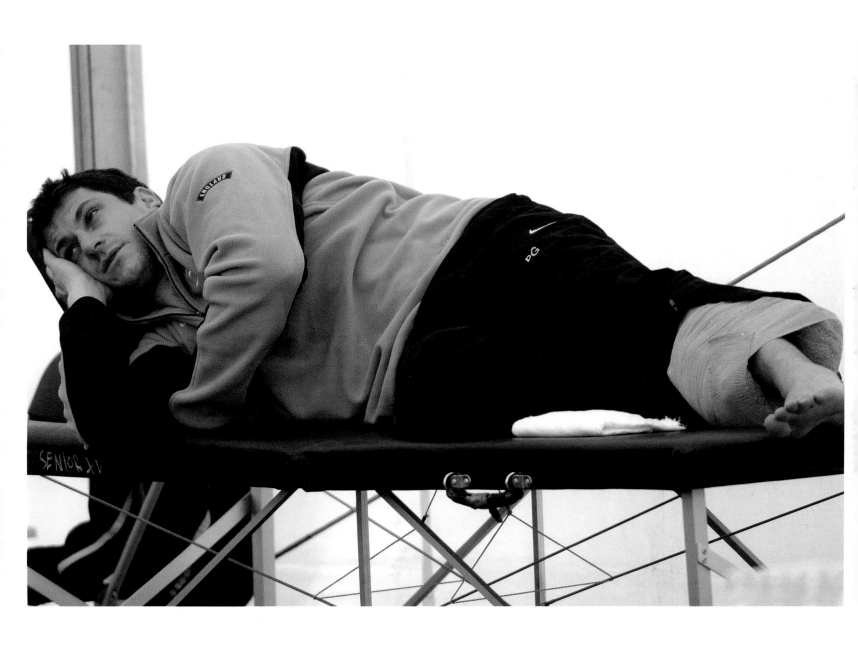

Paul Grayson on the treatment table.
An injured calf kept him out of the last
two matches of the Six Nations'
campaign, and gave Olly Barkley
his chance.

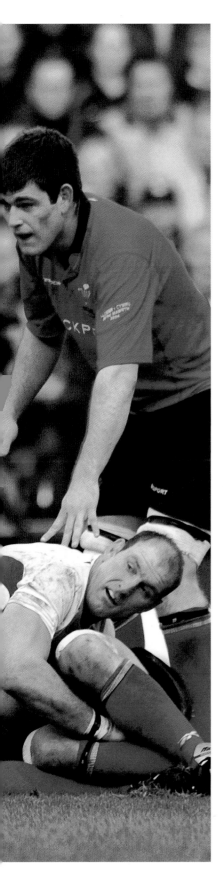

Left Matt Dawson clears the ball from the base of a ruck during the match against Wales.

Above Sir Clive Woodward celebrates an England try during the Six Nations' victory over Wales.

Left An England fan with a bugle at Twickenham for the England v Wales match.

Above New fly-half Olly Barkley lines up a penalty kick against Wales.

Above Ben Cohen fights to get over the tryline and score despite attentions of Jonathan Thomas and Gareth Thomas. Cohen scored two tries and England won 31–21.

Right Mike Tindall is tackled by Tom Shanklin and loses the ball.

Above Part of Matt Dawson's warm-up routine.

Right Olly Barkley practices his kicking at Pennyhill Park.

Left Olly Barkley tries to get through a tackle from Serge Betsen of France in the Six Nations' Championship decider at the Stade de France, Paris.

Above Imanol Harinordoquy gets a pass away before a tackle from Joe Worsley.

Left Ben Kay appeals to the referee.

Above The England mascot Peter Cross during England's poor first half in Paris.

Ben Cohen, Lawrence Dallaglio and
Josh Lewsey applaud France's Grand
Slam after the Six Nations' match.
France won the match 24–21.

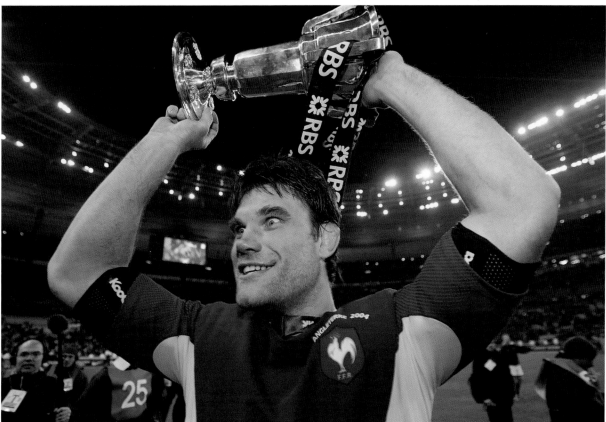

Above France's fly-half Frédéric Michalak celebrates victory for Les Bleus.

Right France captain Fabien Pelous lifts the Six Nations' Championship trophy after the victory over England.

England are named Laureus World Team of the Year at the World Sports Awards in Estoril, Portugal – Neil Back, Martin Johnson and Ben Kay collect the award (right).

Statistics
England Tests June 2003–May 2004

Summer Tour

Westpac Stadium, Wellington, 14 June 2003
New Zealand 13 England 15 (attendance 43,000)

New Zealand	England
15 D Howlett	15 J Lewsey
14 J Rokocoko	14 J Robinson
13 M Nonu	13 W Greenwood
12 T Umaga	12 M Tindall
11 C Ralph	11 B Cohen
10 C Spencer	10 J Wilkinson
9 J Marshall	9 K Bracken
1 D Hewett	1 G Rowntree
2 A Oliver	2 S Thompson
3 G Somerville	3 J Leonard
4 C Jack	4 M Johnson (capt)
5 A Williams	5 B Kay
6 R Thorne (capt)	6 R Hill
7 R McCaw	7 N Back
8 R So'oialo	8 L Dallaglio
16 K Mealamu (replaced Oliver, 61 minutes)	16 D West (not used)
17 C Hoeft (not used)	17 P Vickery (Leonard 40)
18 B Thorn (not used)	18 S Borthwick (not used)
19 J Collins (So'oialo 80)	19 J Worsley (Hill 80)
20 S Devine (not used)	20 A Gomarsall (not used)
21 D Carter (not used)	21 P Grayson (not used)
22 M Muliaina (Rokocoko 80)	22 D Luger (Lewsey 80)

Scorers T: Howlett; C: Spencer; P: Spencer 2

Scorers P: Wilkinson 4; DG: Wilkinson

Telstra Dome, Melbourne, 21 June 2003
Australia 14 England 25 (54,368)

Australia	England
15 C Latham	15 J Lewsey
14 W Sailor	14 J Robinson
13 M Turinui	13 W Greenwood
12 S Kefu	12 M Tindall
11 J Roff	11 B Cohen
10 N Grey	10 J Wilkinson
9 G Gregan (capt)	9 K Bracken
1 B Young	1 T Woodman
2 J Paul	2 S Thompson
3 P Noriega	3 P Vickery
4 D Giffin	4 M Johnson (capt)
5 N Sharpe	5 B Kay
6 D Lyons	6 R Hill
7 P Waugh	7 N Back
8 T Kefu	8 L Dallaglio
16 B Cannon (Paul 54)	16 M Regan (not used)
17 B Darwin (Noriega 69)	17 J Leonard (not used)
18 D Vickerman (Sharpe 45)	18 S Borthwick (Kay 66, 73)
19 D Heenan (not used)	19 J Worsley (Hill 54)
20 C Whitaker (not used)	20 M Dawson (Bracken 54)
21 M Rogers (Turinui 60)	21 A King (not used)
22 L Tuqiri (Grey 69)	22 D Luger (not used)

Scorers T: Sailor; P: Roff 3

Scorers T: Greenwood, Tindall, Cohen; C: Wilkinson 2; P: Wilkinson 2

Rugby World Cup Warm-ups

Millennium Stadium, Cardiff, 23 August 2003
Wales 9 England 43 (60,000)

Wales	England
15 R Williams	15 D Scarbrough
14 M Jones	14 D Luger
13 M Taylor	13 J Noon
12 S Parker	12 S Abbott
11 Gareth Thomas	11 J Simpson-Daniel
10 S Jones (capt)	10 A King
9 G Cooper	9 A Gomarsall
1 I Thomas	1 J Leonard (capt)
2 R McBryde	2 M Regan
3 G Jenkins	3 J White
4 R Sidoli	4 S Shaw
5 C Wyatt	5 D Grewcock
6 C Charvis	6 M Corry
7 M Williams	7 L Moody
8 D Jones	8 J Worsley
16 G Williams (McBryde 61)	16 D West (Regan 37)
17 A Jones (Jenkins 72)	17 W Green (White 72)
18 J Thomas (Wyatt 62)	18 S Borthwick (Shaw 11–16)
19 Gavin Thomas (D Jones 72)	19 A Sanderson (Moody 62)
20 M Phillips (not used)	20 A Healey (not used)
21 T Shanklin (not used)	21 D Walder (King 71)
22 G Henson (not used)	22 O Smith (Luger 56)

Scorers P: S Jones 3

Scorers T: Moody, Luger, Worsley, Abbott, West; C: King 2, Walder; P: King 3; DG: King

---

Rugby World Cup 2003

Stade Vélodrome, Marseilles, 30 August 2003
France 17 England 16 (52,000)

France	England
15 N Brusque	15 I Balshaw
14 A Rougerie	14 J Lewsey
13 Y Jauzion	13 O Smith
12 D Traille	12 M Tindall
11 C Dominici	11 B Cohen
10 F Michalak	10 P Grayson
9 F Galthié (capt)	9 A Healey
1 J-J Crenca	1 G Rowntree
2 Y Bru	2 D West (capt)
3 S Marconnet	3 J White
4 F Pelous	4 S Borthwick
5 J Thion	5 D Grewcock
6 S Betsen	6 M Corry
7 O Magne	7 L Moody
8 I Harinordoquy	8 A Sanderson
16 R Ibanez (Bru 55)	16 S Thompson (West 50)
17 O Milloud (Crenca 67)	17 J Leonard (1–3; Rowntree 60)
18 D Auradou (Thion 65)	18 S Shaw (Borthwick 60)
19 S Chabal (Magne 76)	19 L Moody (Corry 57)
20 P Tabacco (Betsen 65)	20 M Dawson (Bracken 34)
21 X Garbajosa (not used)	21 P Grayson (Wilkinson 43)
22 B Liebenberg (Traille 54)	22 J Noon (Balshaw 54)

Scorers T: Brusque; P: Michalak 3; DG: Michalak

Scorers T: Tindall; C: Grayson; P: Grayson 3

Twickenham, 6 September 2003
England 45 France 14 (75,000)

England	France
15 J Robinson	15 C Poitrenaud
14 I Balshaw	14 X Garbajosa
13 W Greenwood	13 Y Jauzion
12 S Abbott	12 B Liebenberg
11 B Cohen	11 C Dominici
10 J Wilkinson	10 G Merceron
9 K Bracken	9 D Yachvili
1 T Woodman	1 O Milloud
2 S Thompson	2 R Ibanez (capt)
3 J White	3 J-B Poux
4 M Johnson (capt)	4 D Auradou
5 B Kay	5 O Brouzet
6 R Hill	6 P Tabacco
7 N Back	7 S Chabal
8 M Corry	8 C Labit
16 D West (Thompson 73)	16 Y Bru (Ibanez 70)
17 J Leonard (White 63)	17 S Marconnet (Milloud 62)
18 S Shaw (Johnson 43)	18 F Pelous (not used)
19 L Moody (Corry 57)	19 I Harinordoquy (Tabacco 64)
20 M Dawson (Bracken 34)	20 O Magne (Chabal 50)
21 P Grayson (Wilkinson 43)	21 F Michalak (not used)
22 J Lewsey (Abbott 60)	22 A Rougerie (Dominici 40)

Scorers T: Cohen 2, Robinson, Balshaw, Lewsey; C: Wilkinson 3, Grayson; P: Wilkinson 4

Scorers T: Rougerie; P: Merceron 2; DG: Jauzion

Pool C

Subiaco Oval, Perth, 12 October 2003
England 84 Georgia 6 (25,501)

England	Georgia
15 J Lewsey	15 B Khamashuridze
14 J Robinson	14 M Urjukashvili
13 W Greenwood	13 T Zibzibadze
12 M Tindall	12 I Giorgadze
11 B Cohen	11 V Katsadze (capt)
10 J Wilkinson	10 P Jimsheladze
9 M Dawson	9 I Abuseridze
1 T Woodman	1 G Shvelidze
2 S Thompson	2 A Giorgadze
3 P Vickery	3 A Margvelashvili
4 M Johnson (capt)	4 Z Mchedlishvili
5 B Kay	5 V Didebulidze
6 R Hill	6 G Labadze
7 N Back	7 G Yachvili
8 L Dallaglio	8 G Chkhaidze
16 M Regan (Thompson 40)	16 D Dadunashvili (Giorgadze 73)
17 J Leonard (Woodman 29–30; Vickery 50)	17 S Nikolaenko (Margvelashvili 40)
18 D Grewcock (not used)	18 V Nadiradze (Didebulidze 44–46, 50)
19 L Moody (Hill 50)	19 D Bolgashvili (Yachvili 66)
20 A Gomarsall (Dawson 36)	20 M Kvirikashvili (Jimsheladze 75)
21 P Grayson (Wilkinson 46)	21 I Machkhaneli (Chkhaidze 79)
22 D Luger (Tindall 36)	22 B Khekhelashvili (Khamashuridze 75)

Scorers T: Greenwood 2, Cohen 2, Tindall, Dawson, Thompson, Back, Dallaglio, Regan, Robinson, Luger; C: Wilkinson 5, Grayson 4; P: Wilkinson 2

Scorers P: Urjukashvili, Jimsheladze

Subiaco Oval, Perth, 18 October 2003
South Africa 6 England 25 (attendance 38,834)

South Africa	England
15 J van der Westhuyzen	15 J Lewsey
14 A Willemse	14 J Robinson
13 J Muller	13 W Greenwood
12 DW Barry	12 M Tindall
11 T Delport	11 B Cohen
10 L Koen	10 J Wilkinson
9 J van der Westhuizen	9 K Bracken
1 C Bezuidenhout	1 T Woodman
2 D Coetzee	2 S Thompson
3 R Bands	3 P Vickery
4 B Botha	4 M Johnson (capt)
5 V Matfield	5 B Kay
6 C Krige (capt)	6 L Moody
7 J van Niekerk	7 N Back
8 J Smith	8 L Dallaglio
16 J Smit (Coetzee 44–50, 60)	16 D West (not used)
17 L Sephaka (Bands 7–14, 69)	17 J Leonard (Woodman 73)
18 S Boome (not used)	18 M Corry (not used)
19 D Rossouw (not used)	19 J Worsley (Back 46–50)
20 N de Kock (not used)	20 A Gomarsall (not used)
21 D Hougaard (Koen 69)	21 P Grayson (not used)
22 W Greeff (not used)	22 D Luger (Tindall 71)

Scorers P: Koen 2

Scorers T: Greenwood; C: Wilkinson; P: Wilkinson 4; DG: Wilkinson 2

Telstra Dome, Melbourne, 26 October 2003
England 35 Samoa 22 (50,647)

England	Samoa
15 J Robinson	15 T Vili
14 I Balshaw	14 L Fa'atau
13 S Abbott	13 T Fanolua
12 M Tindall	12 B Lima
11 B Cohen	11 S Tagicakibau
10 J Wilkinson	10 E Va'a
9 M Dawson	9 S So'oialo
1 J Leonard	1 K Lealamanu'a
2 M Regan	2 J Meredith
3 J White	3 J Tomuli
4 M Johnson (capt)	4 O Palepoi
5 B Kay	5 L Lafaiali'i
6 J Worsley	6 P Poulos
7 N Back	7 M Fa'asavalu
8 L Dallaglio	8 S Sititi (capt)
16 S Thompson (Regan 48)	16 M Schwalger (Meredith 76)
17 P Vickery (White 48)	17 S Lemalu (Tomuli 53)
18 M Corry (not used)	18 K Viliamu (Poulos 62)
19 L Moody (Worsley 48)	19 D Tuiavi'i (Lafaiali'i 65)
20 A Gomarsall (not used)	20 D Tyrell (So'oialo 76)
21 M Catt (Abbott 70)	21 D Rasmussen (Fanolua 46)
22 D Luger (not used)	22 D Feaunati (Tagicakibau 72)

Scorers T: Back, penalty try, Balshaw, Vickery; C: Wilkinson 3; P: Wilkinson 2; DG: Wilkinson

Scorers T: Sititi; C: Va'a; P: Va'a 5

Suncorp Stadium, Brisbane, 2 November 2003
England 111 Uruguay 13 (46,233)

England	Uruguay
15 J Lewsey	15 J Menchaca
14 I Balshaw	14 J Pastore
13 S Abbott	13 D Aguirre (capt)
12 M Catt	12 J de Freitas
11 D Luger	11 J Viana
10 P Grayson	10 S Aguirre
9 A Gomarsall	9 J Campomar
1 J Leonard	1 E Berruti
2 D West	2 D Lamelas
3 P Vickery (capt)	3 P Lemoine
4 M Corry	4 JC Bado
5 D Grewcock	5 JM Alvarez
6 J Worsley	6 N Brignoni
7 L Moody	7 N Grille
8 L Dallaglio	8 R Capo
16 S Thompson (not used)	16 JA Perez (Lamelas 56)
17 J White (Vickery 52)	17 R Sanchez (Berruti 44)
18 M Johnson (Corry 44)	18 G Storace (Lemoine 68)
19 B Kay (not used)	19 J Alzueta (Alvarez 52)
20 K Bracken (Gomarsall 62)	20 M Gutierrez (Grille 44)
21 W Greenwood (Grayson 62)	21 E Caffera (Menchaca 71)
22 J Robinson (Balshaw 44)	22 D Reyes (De Freitas 5–9, 36–40; Viana 53)

Scorers T: Greenwood, Moody, Balshaw 2, Catt 2, Lewsey 5, Gomarsall 2, Luger, Abbott, Robinson 2; C: Grayson 11, Catt 2

Scorers T: Lemoine; C: Menchaca; P: Menchaca 2

Quarter-final

Suncorp Stadium, Brisbane, 9 November 2003
England 28 Wales 17 (45,252)

England	Wales
15 J Robinson	15 G Thomas
14 D Luger	14 M Jones
13 W Greenwood	13 M Taylor
12 M Tindall	12 I Harris
11 B Cohen	11 S Williams
10 J Wilkinson	10 S Jones
9 M Dawson	9 G Cooper
1 J Leonard	1 I Thomas
2 S Thompson	2 R McBryde
3 P Vickery	3 A Jones
4 M Johnson (capt)	4 B Cockbain
5 B Kay	5 R Sidoli
6 L Moody	6 Dafydd Jones
7 N Back	7 C Charvis (capt)
8 L Dallaglio	8 J Thomas
16 D West (not used)	16 M Davies (McBryde 64)
17 T Woodman (Leonard 45)	17 G Jenkins (A Jones 28)
18 S Shaw (not used)	18 G Llewellyn (Cockbain 48)
19 J Worsley (not used)	19 M Williams (J Thomas 57)
20 K Bracken (Dawson 67)	20 D Peel (Cooper 64)
21 M Catt (Luger 40)	21 C Sweeney (S Jones 59–71)
22 S Abbott (Greenwood 53)	22 K Morgan (not used)

Scorers T: Greenwood; C: Wilkinson; P: Wilkinson 6; DG: Wilkinson

Scorers T: S Jones, Charvis, M Williams; C: Harris

Semi-final

Telstra Stadium, Sydney, 16 November 2003
France 7 England 24 (82,346)

France	England
15 N Brusque	15 J Lewsey
14 A Rougerie	14 J Robinson
13 T Marsh	13 W Greenwood
12 Y Jauzion	12 M Catt
11 C Dominici	11 B Cohen
10 F Michalak	10 J Wilkinson
9 F Galthié (capt)	9 M Dawson
1 J-J Crenca	1 T Woodman
2 R Ibanez	2 S Thompson
3 S Marconnet	3 P Vickery
4 F Pelous	4 M Johnson (capt)
5 J Thion	5 B Kay
6 S Betsen	6 R Hill
7 O Magne	7 N Back
8 I Harinordoquy	8 L Dallaglio
16 Y Bru (not used)	16 D West (Thompson 79)
17 O Milloud (Crenca 62)	17 J Leonard (Vickery 4–5)
18 D Auradou (not used)	18 M Corry (not used)
19 C Labit (Betsen 63)	19 L Moody (Hill 73)
20 G Merceron (Michalak 63)	20 K Bracken (Dawson 70)
21 D Traille (not used)	21 M Tindall (Catt 68)
22 C Poitrenaud (Dominici 33)	22 I Balshaw (not used)

Scorers T: Betsen; C: Michalak

Scorers P: Wilkinson 5; DG: Wilkinson 3

Final

Telstra Stadium, Sydney, 22 November 2003
Australia 17 England 20 (aet; full-time 14–14) (83,500)

Australia	England
15 M Rogers	15 J Lewsey
14 W Sailor	14 J Robinson
13 S Mortlock	13 W Greenwood
12 E Flatley	12 M Tindall
11 L Tuqiri	11 B Cohen
10 S Latkham	10 J Wilkinson
9 G Gregan (capt)	9 M Dawson
1 B Young	1 T Woodman
2 B Cannon	2 S Thompson
3 A Baxter	3 P Vickery
4 J Harrison	4 M Johnson (capt)
5 N Sharpe	5 B Kay
6 G Smith	6 R Hill
7 P Waugh	7 N Back
8 D Lyons	8 L Dallaglio
16 J Paul (Cannon 57)	16 D West (not used)
17 M Dunning (Young 93)	17 J Leonard (Vickery 81)
18 D Giffin (Sharpe 48)	18 M Corry (not used)
19 M Cockbain (Lyons 57)	19 L Moody (Hill 94)
20 C Whitaker (not used)	20 K Bracken (not used)
21 M Giteau (Larkham 19–31, 56–64, 86–94)	21 M Catt (Tindall 79)
22 J Roff (Sailor 71)	22 I Balshaw (Lewsey 86)

Scorers T: Tuqiri; P: Flatley 4

Scorers T: Robinson; P: Wilkinson 4; DG: Wilkinson

Rugby World Cup 2003 Top Points Scorers

Player	Country	Matches	Tries	Cons	Pens	Drops	Total
Jonny Wilkinson	Eng	6	0	10	23	8	113
Frédéric Michalak	Fra	6	2	18	18	1	103
Elton Flatley	Aus	6	1	16	21	0	100
Leon MacDonald	NZ	7	4	20	5	0	75
Chris Paterson	Sco	5	3	7	13	1	71
Mat Rogers	Aus	7	5	16	0	0	57
Mike Hercus	USA	4	2	7	9	0	51
Rima Wakarua	Ita	3	0	4	14	0	50
Earl Va'a	Sam	4	1	10	8	0	49
Daniel Carter	NZ	5	2	19	0	0	48
Derick Hougaard	SA	5	2	10	5	1	48
Nicky Little	Fij	4	0	6	11	0	45
Toru Kurihara	Jap	4	1	4	9	0	40
Stephen Jones	Wal	4	1	5	7	0	36
Doug Howlett	NZ	7	7	0	0	0	35
Mils Muliaina	NZ	7	7	0	0	0	35
Gonzalo Quesada	Arg	3	0	9	4	1	33
Paul Grayson	Eng	2	0	15	0	0	30
Iestyn Harris	Wal	4	0	9	4	0	30
Ronan O'Gara	Ire	5	0	9	4	0	30
Joe Rokocoko	NZ	5	6	0	0	0	30
David Humphreys	Ire	4	0	7	5	0	29

Rugby World Cup 2003 Top Try Scorers

Player	Country	Matches	Tries
Doug Howlett	NZ	7	7
Mils Muliaina	NZ	7	7
Joe Rokocoko	NZ	5	6
Will Greenwood	Eng	6	5
Chris Latham	Aus	1	5
Josh Lewsey	Eng	5	5
Mat Rogers	Aus	7	5
Lote Tuqiri	Aus	7	5
Pablo Bouza	Arg	2	4
Christophe Dominici	Fra	5	4
Martin Gaitan	Arg	2	4
Matt Giteau	Aus	6	4
Leon MacDonald	NZ	7	4
Stirling Mortlock	Aus	5	4
Caleb Ralph	NZ	4	4
Jason Robinson	Eng	7	4
Carlos Spencer	NZ	7	4

Zurich World Champions Challenge (caps not awarded)

Twickenham, 20 December 2003
England XV 42 New Zealand Barbarians 17 (75,000)

England XV	New Zealand Barbarians
15 J Robinson	15 J Muller
14 J Simpson-Daniel	14 R Gear
13 O Smith	13 K Lowen
12 S Abbott	12 D Gibson
11 B Cohen	11 D Albanese
10 P Grayson	10 G Jackson
9 A Gomarsall	9 D Lee
1 T Woodman	1 T Woodcock
2 A Titterrell	2 A Hore
3 M Stevens	3 D Manu
4 S Shaw	4 T Flavell
5 D Grewcock	5 S Maling
6 M Corry	6 T Randell (capt)
7 R Hill (capt)	7 J Blackie
8 J Worsley	8 X Rush

16 A Long (not used)
17 A Sheridan (Woodman 54)
18 H Vyvyan (Hill 60)
19 P Sanderson (Hill 6–20; Corry 54)
20 K Bracken (Gomarsall 63)
21 B Gollings (Abbott 79)
22 M Tindall (Smith 54)

16 A Tiatia (Hore 48)
17 M Hurter (Manu 65)
18 N Maxwell (Maling 58)
19 S Harding (Rush 38)
20 B Willis (Lee 60)
21 T Vili (Gibson 65)
22 E Taione (Gear 73)

Scorers T: Cohen 2, Grayson, Stevens, Simpson-Daniel, Tindall; C: Grayson 3; P: Grayson 2

Scorers T: Flavell, Lowen; C: Jackson 2 ; P: Jackson

RBS Six Nations Championship 2004

Stadio Flaminio, Rome, 15 February 2004
Italy 9 England 50 (28,500)

Italy	England
15 A Masi	15 I Balshaw
14 N Mazzucato	14 J Lewsey
13 C Stoica	13 W Greenwood
12 M Dallan	12 J Robinson
11 D Dallan	11 B Cohen
10 R Wakarua	10 P Grayson
9 P Griffen	9 A Gomarsall
1 A lo Cicero	1 T Woodman
2 F Ongaro	2 S Thompson
3 M Castrogiovanni	3 P Vickery
4 S Dellape	4 D Grewcock
5 M Bortolami	5 B Kay
6 A de Rossi (capt)	6 J Worsley
7 A Persico	7 R Hill
8 S Parisse	8 L Dallaglio (capt)

16 C Festuccia (Ongaro 63)
17 S Perugini (Castrogiovanni 69)
18 C Checchinato (Dellape 64)
19 S Orlando (not used)
20 S Picone (not used)
21 R de Marigny (M Dallan 69)
22 Mirco Bergamasco (Mazzucato 47)

16 M Regan (Thompson 67)
17 J Leonard (Vickery 69)
18 S Shaw (Grewcock 38–40, 58)
19 C Jones (Worsley 63)
20 M Dawson (Gomarsall 63)
21 O Barkley (Grayson 69)
22 H Paul (Robinson 52–58; Balshaw 58)

Scorers P: Wakarua 2; DG: Wakarua

Scorers T: Balshaw, Robinson 3, Lewsey, Grayson, Jones; C: Grayson 3; P: Grayson 3

Murrayfield, Edinburgh, 21 February 2004
Scotland 13 England 35 (67,500)

Scotland	England
15 B Hinshelwood	15 I Balshaw
14 S Danielli	14 J Lewsey
13 T Philip	13 W Greenwood
12 B Laney	12 J Robinson
11 S Webster	11 B Cohen
10 C Paterson (capt)	10 P Grayson
9 C Cusiter	9 A Gomarsall
1 T Smith	1 T Woodman
2 G Bulloch	2 S Thompson
3 B Douglas	3 P Vickery
4 S Murray	4 D Grewcock
5 S Grimes	5 B Kay
6 J White	6 C Jones
7 C Mather	7 R Hill
8 S Taylor	8 L Dallaglio (capt)

16 R Russell (Bulloch 68)
17 G Kerr (Douglas 47)
18 N Hines (Grimes 55)
19 A Hogg (Mather 20)
20 M Blair (Cusiter 53)
21 D Parks (Danielli 79)
22 A Henderson (Philip 17–24; Hinshelwood 40)

16 M Regan (not used)
17 J Leonard (not used)
18 S Shaw (Kay 58)
19 A Sanderson (not used)
20 M Dawson (Gomarsall 56)
21 O Barkley (not used)
22 H Paul (Greenwood 79)

Scorers T: Danielli; C: Paterson; P: Paterson 2

Scorers T: Cohen, Balshaw, Lewsey, Grewcock; C: Grayson 3; P: Grayson 3

Twickenham, 6 March 2004
England 13 Ireland 19 (75,000)

England	Ireland
15 I Balshaw	15 G Dempsey
14 J Lewsey	14 S Horgan
13 W Greenwood	13 B O'Driscoll (capt)
12 J Robinson	12 G D'Arcy
11 B Cohen	11 T Howe
10 P Grayson	10 R O'Gara
9 M Dawson	9 P Stringer
1 T Woodman	1 R Corrigan
2 S Thompson	2 S Byrne
3 P Vickery	3 J Hayes
4 S Borthwick	4 M O'Kelly
5 B Kay	5 P O'Connell
6 J Worsley	6 S Easterby
7 R Hill	7 K Gleeson
8 L Dallaglio (capt)	8 A Foley

16 M Regan (Thompson 60)
17 M Stevens (not used)
18 C Jones (Worsley 53)
19 N Back (not used)
20 A Gomarsall (not used)
21 O Barkley (Grayson 55–66)
22 J Simpson-Daniel (Balshaw 53)

16 F Sheahan (not used)
17 S Best (not used)
18 G Longwell (not used)
19 V Costello (not used)
20 G Easterby (not used)
21 D Humphreys (not used)
22 K Maggs (Dempsey 72)

Scorers T: Dawson; C: Grayson; P: Grayson 2

Scorers T: Dempsey; C: O'Gara; P: O'Gara 4

Twickenham, 20 March 2004
England 31 Wales 21 (75,000)

England	Wales
15 J Robinson	15 G Thomas
14 J Lewsey	14 R Williams
13 W Greenwood	13 M Taylor
12 M Tindall	12 T Shanklin
11 B Cohen	11 S Williams
10 O Barkley	10 S Jones
9 M Dawson	9 G Cooper
1 T Woodman	1 Duncan Jones
2 S Thompson	2 R McBryde
3 P Vickery	3 G Jenkins
4 D Grewcock	4 B Cockbain
5 B Kay	5 M Owen
6 C Jones	6 J Thomas
7 R Hill	7 C Charvis (capt)
8 L Dallaglio (capt)	8 Dafydd Jones

16 M Regan (not used)
17 J White (Vickery 73)
18 S Borthwick (not used)
19 J Worsley (Jones 40)
20 A Gomarsall (not used)
21 M Catt (Greenwood 78)
22 J Simpson-Daniel (not used)

16 M Davies (not used)
17 B Evans (Jenkins 65–72)
18 G Llewellyn (Cockbain 28)
19 M Williams (J Thomas 68)
20 D Peel (Cooper 61)
21 C Sweeney (Taylor 69)
22 Jamie Robinson (not used)

Scorers T: Cohen 2, Worsley; C: Barkley 2; P: Barkley 4

Scorers T: Taylor, G Thomas; C: S Jones; P: S Jones 3

Stade de France, Paris, 27 March 2004
France 24 England 21 (80,000)

France	England
15 N Brusque	15 J Robinson
14 P Elhorga	14 J Lewsey
13 Y Jauzion	13 W Greenwood
12 D Traille	12 M Tindall
11 C Dominici	11 B Cohen
10 F Michalak	10 O Barkley
9 D Yachvili	9 M Dawson
1 S Marconnet	1 T Woodman
2 W Servat	2 S Thompson
3 P de Villiers	3 P Vickery
4 F Pelous (capt)	4 D Grewcock
5 P Papé	5 B Kay
6 S Betsen	6 J Worsley
7 O Magne	7 R Hill
8 I Harinordoquy	8 L Dallaglio (capt)

16 Y Bru (Servat 53)
17 J-J Crenca (Marconnet 71)
18 D Auradou (Pelous 78)
19 T Lièvremont (not used)
20 P Mignoni (not used)
21 J Peyrelongue (not used)
22 C Poitrenaud (Jauzion 56)

16 M Regan (not used)
17 J White (Vickery 64)
18 S Borthwick (Grewcock 24)
19 M Corry (not used)
20 A Gomarsall (not used)
21 M Catt (Greenwood 48)
22 J Simpson-Daniel (not used)

Scorers T: Harinordoquy, Yachvili; C: Yachvili; P: Yachvili 4

Scorers T: Cohen, Lewsey; C: Barkley; P: Barkley

RBS Six Nations Championship 2004 Final Table

	P	W	D	L	F	A	Pts
France	5	5	0	0	144	60	10
Ireland	5	4	0	1	128	82	8
England	5	3	0	2	150	86	6
Wales	5	2	0	3	125	116	4
Italy	5	1	0	4	42	152	2
Scotland	5	0	0	5	53	146	0

Miscellaneous Records

▶ With his winning dropped goal against Australia in the Rugby World Cup final, Jonny Wilkinson extended his individual points record total for England to 817 (5 tries, 161 penalty goals, 123 conversions and 21 dropped goals), ahead of Paul Grayson (400) and Rob Andrew (396)

▶ Wilkinson has also scored 36 points for the British & Irish Lions; his 853 points overall in Tests puts him sixth on the worldwide list behind Neil Jenkins (Wales and the Lions, 1090 points), Diego Dominguez (Italy, 983), Andrew Mehrtens (New Zealand, 932), Michael Lynagh (Australia, 911) and Matt Burke (Australia, 866)

▶ Jason Leonard retired from playing at the end of the 2003–04 season, as the world's most capped international. The Harlequins and former Saracens prop made 114 Test appearances for England, and five for the British & Irish Lions

▶ Martin Johnson's 84 caps placed him third behind Leonard and Rory Underwood (85) in the England Test appearance table.

England Caps

Jason Leonard	114	Matt Dawson	62
Rory Underwood	85	Peter Winterbottom	58
Martin Johnson	84	Wade Dooley	55
Will Carling	72	Will Greenwood	52
Rob Andrew	71	Jonny Wilkinson	52
Lawrence Dallaglio	70	Kyran Bracken	51
Richard Hill	68	Austin Healey	51
Neil Back	66		
Jerry Guscott	65	(all records correct to 1 June 2004)	
Brian Moore	64		
Mike Catt	63		

Index

Photographic Credits

2 David Rogers/Getty Images; **5** Darren England/Getty Images; **7** Steve Cuff/Empics; **8** David Rogers/Getty Images; **11** Danni Collier/Offside; **12–13** David Rogers/Getty Images; **14** David Rogers/Getty Images; **15** David Rogers/Getty Images; **17** David Rogers/Getty Images; **18** David Rogers/Getty Images; **21** Greg Wood/AFP/Getty Images; **22** David Rogers/Getty Images; **23** Ross Land/Fotopress; **24** Anthony Phelps/Reuters; **25** Simon Baker/Pro Sport Photos; **26–27** Anthony Phelps/Reuters; **28** Sandra Teddy/Offside; **29** Sandra Teddy/Offside; **30** Stuart Milligan/Reuters; **31** Sean Garnsworthy/Getty Images; **32–33** David Rogers/Getty Images; **34–35** Rick Rycroft/AP; **36** Ryan Pierse/Getty Images; **37** Top William West/AFP/Getty Images; **37** Bottom David Rogers/Getty Images; **38** David Rogers/Getty Images; **39** David Rogers/Getty Images; **40–41** David Rogers/Getty Images; **42** Andrew Fosker; **43** Darren Staples/Reuters; **44** Franck Nataf/Offside; 45 David Rogers/Getty Images; **46** Toby Melville/Reuters; **47** Philippe Laurenson/Reuters; 48 David Rogers/Getty Images; **49** David Rogers/Getty Images; **50–51** David Ashdown; **52** Tom Jenkins; **53** David Ashdown; **54** Toby Melville/Reuters; **55** Mike Hewitt/Getty Images; **56** Stu Williamson; **57** Philip Brown; **58–59** Eddie Keogh; **61** Jon Buckle/Getty Images; **63** Adam Butler/AP; **64–65** Nick Laham/Getty Images; **66** Greg Wood/AFP/Getty Images; **67** Adam Pretty/Getty Images; **69** Chris McGrath/Getty Images; **70** Kieran Doherty/Reuters; **71** Top Kieran Doherty/Reuters; **71** Bottom Kieran Doherty/Reuters; **72** David Rogers/Getty Images; **73** David Rogers/Getty Images; **74** Kieran Doherty/Reuters; **75** Richard Lane/Sportbeat; **76** Eddie Keogh; **77** Adam Butler/AP; **78** Top Eddie Keogh; **78** Bottom David Rogers/Getty Images; **79** Kieran Doherty/Reuters; **80** Adam Butler/AP; **81** Greg Wood/AFP/Getty Images; **82** Pat Scala/Fairfax; **83** Kieran Doherty/Reuters; **84** Greg Wood/AFP/Getty Images; **85** Greg Wood/AFP/Getty Images; **86** Stuart Hannagan/Getty Images; **87** David Rogers/Getty Images; **88** Manuel Blondeau/Corbis; **89** Tony Ashby/AFP/Getty Images; **90** David Rogers/Getty Images; **91** Matthew Impey/Colorsport/Corbis; **92–93** Mark Baker/AP; **94** Richard Lane/Sportbeat; **95** Top David Rogers/Getty Images; **95** Bottom Jon Buckle/Getty Images; **96** Kieran Doherty/Reuters; **97** Adam Butler/AP; **98–99** William West/AFP/Getty Images; **100** Mark Dadswell/Getty Images; **101** Richard Lane/Sportbeat; **102** Nick Laham/Getty Images; **103** Nick Laham/Getty Images; **104** Adam Butler/AP; **105** Eddie Keogh; **106** Top Eddie Keogh; **106** Bottom Greg Wood/AFP/Getty Images; **107** Richard Lane/Sportbeat; **108** Kieran Doherty/Reuters; **109** Top Greg Wood/AFP/Getty Images; **109** Bottom left Adam Butler/AP; **109** Bottom right Greg Wood/AFP/Getty Images; **110** Adrees Latif/Reuters; **111** Christophe Simon/AFP/Getty Images; **112–113** Cameron Spencer/Getty Images; **114** Jon Buckle/Getty Images; **115** David Rogers/Getty Images; **116–117** Darren England/Getty Images; **118** Eddie Keogh; **119** Christophe Simon/AFP/Getty Images; **120–121** Tom Jenkins; **123** Gareth Copley/PA; **124** Gareth Copley/PA; **126–127** David Davies/PA; **128** David Davies/PA; **131** David Davies/PA; **132** Marc Aspland; **133** Mike Hutchings/Reuters/Corbis; **134** Tom Jenkins; **135** Adam Butler/AP; **136** Adam Butler/AP; **137** Peter Parks/AFP/Getty Images; **138** Mark Pain; **139** Greg White/Reuters; **140–141** Tom Jenkins; **142** Adam Pretty/Getty Images; **143** Eddie Keogh; **144** Steve Holland/AP; **145** Adam Pretty/Getty Images; **146–147** Paul Seiser; **148–149** Paul Seiser; **150** Jonathon Wood/Getty Images; **151** Marc Aspland; **152** Marc Aspland; **153** David Gray/Reuters; **154** David Davies/PA; **155** Marc Aspland; **156** Greg Wood/AFP/Getty Images; **157** Marc Aspland; 158 Kieran Doherty/Reuters; **159** Marc Aspland; **160** Jim Keogh; **161** Manuel Blondeau/Corbis; **162** Kieran Doherty/Reuters; **163** Daniel Berehulak/Getty Images; **164** Manuel Blondeau/Corbis; **165** Greg Wood/AFP/Getty Images; **166** Eddie Keogh; **167** Mark Baker/AP; **168–169** Tom Jenkins; **170** Andrew Cornega/Offside; **171** Mark Nolan/Getty Images; **172** Jon Buckle/Getty Images; **173** Matthew Impey/Colorsport/ Corbis; **174–175** Marc Aspland; **176** Steve Holland/Sportsbeat; **177** Tom Jenkins; **178–179** David Rogers/Getty Images; **180** Tim Clayton/Fairfax; **181** Phil Walter/Fotopress; **182** Tom Jenkins; **183** Kieran Doherty/Reuters; **184** David Rogers/Getty Images; **185** Tom Jenkins; **186–187** David Rogers/Getty Images; **188** Kieran Doherty/Reuters; **189** David Davies/PA; **190–191** Phil Gray; 192 Eddie Keogh; 193 David Rogers/Getty Images; 194 Matthew Impey/Colorsport/Corbis; **195** Steve Christo/Fairfax; **196** Left Daniel Berehulak/Getty Images; **196** Right Adam Pretty/Getty Images; **197** Matthew Impey/Colorsport/Corbis; **198–199** Nick Laham/Getty Images; **200** Marc Aspland; **201** Dave Rogers/Getty Images; **202** Tom Jenkins; **203** Top Craig Golding/Fairfax; **203** Bottom Craig Golding/Fairfax; **204–205** David Davies/PA; **206** Christophe Simon/AFP/Getty Images; **207** Nicolas Luttiau/Offside; **208** David Rogers/Getty Images; **209** Tom Jenkins; **210** Adam Pretty/Getty Images ; **211** Nick Laham/Getty Images ; **212–213** David Rogers/Getty Images; **214** Tom Jenkins; **215** Kieran Doherty/Reuters; **216–217** Joe Mann/Offside; **218** Chris McGrath/Getty Images; **219** Richard Lane/Sportsbeat; **220** Jon Buckle/Getty Images; **221** Richard Lane/Sportsbeat; **222** Adrees Latif/Reuters; **223** Simon Baker/Reuters; **224–225** Tom Jenkins; **226** Manuel Blondeau/Corbis; **227** Eddie Keogh; **228** Eddie Keogh; **229** Bernard Papon/Offside; **230** Bernard Papon/Offside; **231** Bernard Papon/Offside; **232–233** Mark Pain; **234** Steve Christo/Fairfax; **235** Andy Hooper; **236–237** Tom Jenkins; **238** David Roger/Getty Images; **239** David Gibson; Page **240–241** Marc Aspland; **242–243** David Davies/PA; **244** Nick Laham/Getty Images; **245** Stephen Hird/Reuters; **247** Eddie Keogh; **248** Paul Miller/AAP; **251** David Rogers/Getty Images; **252–253** Ryan Pierse/Getty Images; **254** Eddie Keogh; **255** Daniel Berehulak/Getty Images; **256** Richard Lewis/AP; **257** Veronique de Viguerie/Reuters; **258** Ian Waldie/Getty Images; **259** Sean Dempsey/PA; **260** Lee Besford/Reuters; **261** David Davies/PA; **262** Adrian Dennis/AFP/Getty Images; **263** Adrian Dennis/AFP/Getty Images; **264** Scott Barbour/Getty Images; **265** Adrian Dennis/AFP/Getty Images; **266–267** Kirsty Wigglesworth/PA; **268** David Rogers/Getty Images; **269** Paul Gilham/Getty Images; **270** Mike Finn–Kelcey/Reuters; **271** Nigel French/Empics; **272** David Rogers/Getty Images; **273** Richard Lane/Sportsbeat; **274–275** Philip Brown; **276** Simon Bellis/Reuters; **277** Kieran Doherty/Reuters; **279** Jim Watson/AFP/Getty Images; **280–281** Frank Coppi; **283** Philip Brown; **284** Philip Brown; **286** Neil Plumb/Raymonds; **287** Russell Cheyne; **288** Dylan Martinez/Reuters; **289** Marc Aspland; **290–291** Marc Aspland; **292** Dylan Martinez/Reuters; **293** Paolo Cocco/AFP/Getty Images; **294** David Rogers/Getty Images; **295** Frank Coppi; **296** David Rogers/Getty Images; **297** Ian Hodgson/Reuters; **298** Jeff J Mitchell/Reuters; **299** David Rogers/Getty Images; **300–301** David Rogers/Getty Images; **302–303** Marc Aspland; **304** Philip Brown; **305** Philip Brown; **306–307** Tommy Hindley/Professional Sport; **308** Toby Melville/Reuters; **309** Mark Leech/Offside; **310** Jamie McDonald/Getty Images; **311** Russell Cheyne; **312** Philip Brown; **313** Andrew Fosker; **314** Philip Brown; **315** Philip Brown; **316** Philip Brown; **317** Russell Cheyne; **318** Eddie Keogh; **319** Toby Melville/Reuters; **320** Frank Coppi; **321** David Rogers/Getty Images; **322** Russell Cheyne; **323** Philip Brown; **324** Philippe Wojazer/Reuters; **325** David Rogers/Getty Images; **326** Ross Kinnaird/Getty Images; **327** Top Martin Bureau/AFP/Getty Images; **327** Bottom David Rogers/Getty Images; **328** David Cannon/Getty Images; **329** Gary M Prior/Getty Images

Acknowledgments

Philip Brown

Gabrielle Allen, Julian Andrews, Vivien Antwi, Marc Aspland, Mark Baker, Simon Baker, Laura Bogard, Vivienne Brar, Adam Butler, Wayne Caba, Russell Cheyne, Tim Clayton, Mick Cleary, Dan Collins, Frank Coppi, David Davies, Nigel Davies, Kieran Doherty, Sarah Edworthy, John Elliott, Tiffinni Field, Mark Fletcher, Andrew Fosker, Brendan Gallagher, David Gibson, Hugh Godwin, Jane Gowman, Phil Gray, Jeff Grout, Ian Heads, Giulia Hetherington, Lynne Hill, Stephen Hird, Steve Holland, Robin Hume, Tom Jenkins, Natalie Jones, Terry Jones, Eddie Keogh, Jim Keogh, David Killick, Sara Kirby, John Knight, Emma Land, Richard Lane, Kim Lee, Mark Leech, Emily Lewis, Maria Lopez-Duran, David Luxton, Rick Mayston, Huw Morgan, Ron Norton, Marina Palmer, Madeleine Penny, Emma Perry, Keith Perry, Anthony Phelps, Robert Philip, David Rogers, Paul Seiser, Phil Sheldon, Martin Smith, Peter Taylor, Richard Tulk-Hart, Phil Walter, Naomi Waters, Tony Waymouth, William West, Stuart Wetherhead, and Kirsty Wigglesworth and to all the photographers who took the brilliant photographs that appear in this book.

Special thanks go to Fiona, Rory, and Emily for all their love and support.

Hugh Godwin

In recalling the facts and feats of England's year, newspaper and magazine libraries were valuable sources of memories and testimony. The official websites of IRB Rugby World Cup 2003 and the RBS Six Nations Championship carried useful statistical data and interviews. Other sources included the BBC television documentary "The Rugby World Cup: England's Story", which utilised footage shot by the squad's video analyst, Tony Biscombe; Matt Dawson's autobiography *Nine Lives* (Collins Willow), and Phil Vickery's DVD/Video "Champion! From Tears to Triumph" (Empire Media Productions). Thanks are also due to my colleagues at the *Independent on Sunday*, to Andy Gomarsall for his description of England's preparations and to Tony Prince, who rode the "Sweet Chariot" home from Sydney.